SECRETS OF THE
INTERIOR LIFE

SECRETS OF THE INTERIOR LIFE

by

LUIS M. MARTINEZ, D.D.

Archbishop of Mexico

TRANSLATED BY

H. J. BEUTLER, C.M., S.T.L.

**St. John's Seminary
Camarillo, Calif.**

B. HERDER BOOK CO.

15 & 17 SOUTH BROADWAY, ST. LOUIS 2, MO.

AND

33 QUEEN SQUARE, LONDON, W. C.

Library of Congress Catalog Card Number: 50-4335

2483

Copyright 1949

B. HERDER BOOK CO.

Reprinted 1958

Vail-Ballou Press, Inc., Binghamton and New York

To the Reader

In Mexico the writings of Archbishop Luis M. Martinez are justly held in high esteem. When I first happened on some of them, I was moved by their deep spirituality and charmed by their simplicity of style, but, particularly, I was amazed to learn that no one had ever attempted to translate them into English.

Feeling that the spiritual riches lodged in the conferences of the distinguished Archbishop merited expression in English, because of the great good that could be effected by a wider diffusion of them to souls yearning after perfection, I decided to undertake the task of rendering his *Simientes Divinas* into my native tongue under the title *Secrets of the Interior Life.*

From first to last the work has been a labor of love. At times, to be sure, I grew discouraged in my attempts to give a fitting English dress to the exquisite Spanish of the Archbishop. The thought, however, of the spiritual good for souls that an English version of one of his works would undoubtedly effect steadied me in my labors.

I have tried always to be faithful to the thought of Archbishop Martinez; and even though I may not have succeeded in giving to the translation the elevated tone of the original, I trust that my modest efforts will, nevertheless, provide profitable spiritual reading for English readers.

If only one person is brought closer to God by his perusal of the present volume, I shall feel amply rewarded for my undertaking; for one of the chief secrets of the interior life is the golden truth that in the very act of bringing others nearer to God we ourselves are invariably drawn closer to Him also.

The Translator

Contents

I

The Sower

▀▀▀▀▀▀▀▀▀▀▀▀▀▀▀▀▀▀▀▀▀▀▀▀▀▀▀▀▀▀▀▀▀▀▀▀▀▀▀

"Behold the sower went forth to sow" [1]

I have seen the enchanting scene. In the exhilaration of the dawn, when the sky is filled with colors and the earth with melodies, the sower goes out to sow his seed. Over the newly turned furrow, over the moist and warm furrow, he walks slowly, rhythmically, with such even gait that he appears to be a mechanical figure. One would say that his eyes gaze not so much on the distance of the horizon as on the vistas of the future; that on his lips is traced the smile of hope; that in dreamy harmony with the delicate canticle of nature, as it comes to life, his spirit dreams of the future, of the abundant harvest that the rich earth will produce.

His hand scatters the wheat with masterly skill; and as the ruddy grains fall upon the black soil, they appear, in the splendor of the rising sun, like a shining fan of gold. One after another the handfuls of wheat are cast upon the ground, while the fields gradually fill with light, and great numbers

[1] Matt. 13:3.

of birds flutter over the newly sown earth—all very black, very talkative, very restless.

The grains of wheat buried in the ground will die, for death is the indispensable condition of life; they will die to live again. From each one of them will rise a sturdy and luxuriant stalk, and from each stalk a multitude of ears rich with grain.

Among the sacred monuments of Hellenic art in the streets of Athens, the center of the ancient civilization, there walks with majesty a man. A heavenly light shines in his eyes, and from his lips there issues, like the exquisite honey of Mount Hybla, words full of depth and unction.

In the bosom of the corrupt Athenian society Socrates sows the seed of the word, the seed of truth. Perhaps it germinates in the depth of his soul because of the supernatural breath of a hidden spirit; perhaps it develops in the mysteriousness of his transcendent rapture; perchance it grows with the warmth of his profound meditations. Who can know?

One day the philosopher went forth, his soul filled with the heavenly seed, and he lavished the golden fan of his word upon the barren furrow. He illuminated many souls, he changed many hearts, he provoked many discussions, while his eyes searched the distance of the centuries, and the smile of an undying hope formed on his lips.

The word of Socrates died to be born again. Through its magic influence Plato and Aristotle arose; and upon them, as in a sturdy and everlasting trunk, the Church grafted, in the Middle Ages, the tremendous scholastic synthesis, the glorious synthesis that will never die.

What force does the human word possess that it thus perdures, that it thus transforms, that it thus extends itself?

God has placed in it life and hope.

From the mysterious bosom of the Father and from the virginal bosom of Mary there came forth, in the midst of the splendors of sanctity, the true sower, the only sower, Jesus.

Upon the ungrateful soil of the human race, whence germinated only thorns and briars, He came to sow His words of eternal life, His seed— the only fruitful seed, the only seed that does not die, because it is the word of God. "The seed is the word of God."

To speak the truth, the seed of the fields and the seed of souls, the wheat of the farmer and the word of Socrates, are always "the word of God," a reflection, an image, an echo of the Word of God. How could fecundity and life come from any other source?

There is only one seed: the word of God. All else is a figure or a resemblance. The biblical phrase, "The sower went forth to sow," is applicable in its full extent to Jesus alone.

For thirty-three years the divine Sower sowed upon the earth. He sowed silently at Nazareth, sweetly on the Mount, lavishly in Tiberias, gloriously on Thabor, ineffably in the Cenacle, sorrowfully in Gethsemane and on Calvary. His seed is one and multiple, as the Sacred Scriptures say: one because it is the Word of God, multiple because in that Word is everything— "by Him all things consist," [2]—light, love, counsel, hope, happiness.

Three divine fruits issued from the divine seed: the Gospel, the Eucharist, the Church: a prodigality of light, a marvel of love, a miracle of strength. And these three fruits prepare for and contain the supreme fruit, eternal life.

How small man appears before the majesty of God!

In the footsteps of the divine Sower there follows an innumerable host of sowers who continue to scatter over the earth the divine seed, one and multiple.

All sow the word, each one in his particular way: virgins are sowers of purity; martyrs, of sacrifice; doctors, of wisdom. Some sow by their preaching, others by their example; some with their labors, others with their tears or their blood.

"What is it that this word-sower would say?" asked the Athenians in the Areopagus upon hearing St. Paul. The Apostle is the type of the sower of the words of life. He covered the earth, scattering abroad his seed. How much weariness, how many dangers, how much suffering he underwent

[2] Col. 1:17.

to achieve the marvel of his great and fruitful sow-
ing!

Nineteen centuries ago he went forth to spread
his seed abroad, and he sows it still; for in these
nineteen centuries the vigorous word of St. Paul
has ever resounded. "The sower went forth to sow
his seed."

I also am a sower, and I go forth to sow my seed,
my very own, which sprang up in the depth of my
heart, which was placed there by Jesus, and which
by Him was blessed and nurtured: the seed of St.
Paul, the seed of Christ, but a seed that has been
made my own. I also go out into the world to scatter
my seed, watering the furrow with my sweat and
my tears.

And as the fertile seed falls upon souls, my spirit
contemplates the horizon of the future; it dreams
of the golden harvest, the most rich harvest that
someone will eventually gather in. May God implant hope and life in my words!

II

Divine Paradoxes

▰▰▰▰▰▰▰▰▰▰▰▰▰▰▰▰▰▰▰▰▰▰▰▰▰▰▰▰▰▰▰▰▰▰▰▰▰▰

There are divine paradoxes in the spiritual life which disconcert not only worldlings, but even pious souls when they are not well instructed, especially with that instruction of the Holy Ghost which is never lacking to souls of good will and of which Sacred Scripture says, "Blessed is the man whom Thou shalt instruct, O Lord: and shalt teach him out of Thy law." [1]

In this chapter I am going to speak on one of the most important and utterly fundamental of these paradoxes.

The spiritual life is indubitably a continual ascent, since perfection consists in union with God, and God stands above all creation. To arrive at God we must ascend; but the paradox that I emphasize lies in this, that the secret of ascending is to descend. St. Augustine, in his inimitable style, thus explains this paradox: "Consider, O Brethren, this great marvel. God is on high: reach up to Him,

[1] Ps. 93:12.

and He flees from you; lower yourself before Him, and He comes down to you." [2]

St. John of the Cross picturesquely teaches the same in the title page of his book, *The Ascent of Mount Carmel*, from which I take only these lines:

> "In order to come to be all,
> Desire in all things to be nothing."

And what is the basis of the marvelous "Little Way" taught to souls in modern times by St. Theresa of the Child Jesus except a simple, sweet, and profound way of descending in order that the soul may be lifted up by the divine power of the very arms of Jesus?

All this and much more that could be quoted is simply a commentary on these words of our Lord: "Everyone that exalteth himself, shall be humbled; and he that humbleth himself, shall be exalted." [3]

This teaching is clear and well known, but it is commonly forgotten in practice, not only by reason of the obstacles that the passions always place in the way when we try to live in conformity to the divine teachings, but also because souls are troubled by this divine paradox, even in their very judgments.

There is, indeed, a natural tendency to judge of divine things by human standards. To this St. Thomas Aquinas attributes our defections from

[2] *Sermo 2 de Ascensione.*
[3] Luke 14:11.

good, for, he says, man "wishes to measure divine things according to the reasons of sensible things." This explains the basis of these paradoxes and the frequent difficulties of souls, even when they know the doctrine.

This descending in order to ascend, which is the foundation of humility, appears natural and human in its first stages; and therefore Jules Lemaitre was able to say: "Humility is not only the most religious but also the most philosophical of the virtues. To resign oneself to be only the little that one is, and to fear to pass the limits of this little, is not that the consummation of wisdom?" [4]

But Christian humility, particularly in its highest perfection, excels philosophical humility as heaven does the earth; and if at first the lowliness of humility finds quarter in the narrow confines of human reason, little by little it overflows such restricted limits and confounds the human spirit.

In the spiritual life souls humble themselves with more or less effort, yet ever retaining the conviction that they must become little; but when they descend to a certain depth, they become dismayed and grow weary of descending. It seems to them that they are being deceived and that the time has now come for them to ascend, because they are not aware that in the way of spirituality one ascends only by descending, and that to arrive at the sum-

---

[4] *Jean Jacques Rousseau,* p. 334.

mit the soul must never weary of going downward. Let this "never" be well understood; for, just as in the beginnings of the purgative way, so also in the heights of the unitive, the one and only secret for ascending is to descend.

With the light of God the soul makes steady progress in seeing its own misery and in sinking down into it; and with each new illumination it seems that its eyes have arrived at the base of its nothingness. But our miserableness has no bottom, and only the grace of God can sound the profound depths of that abyss; for us new revelations of our nothingness always remain, even though we may live a long time and receive torrents of light from God.

We can always descend lower; we can always sink deeper in our misery: and to the measure that we descend, we ascend, because thus we come nearer to God, for one can see God better from below, and thereby more sweetly enjoy His caresses and more intimately experience the charm of His divine presence.

But in the depth of our soul there always remains the tendency to measure divine things with our human standard, and hence with each new revelation of our misery our confusion increases, and we would gladly close our eyes in order not to see: just as certain sick people do not wish to know of their illness because they feel that not to know it is not to have it, as though the knowledge of one's malady were not in itself the beginning of a serious cure.

For this reason souls become dismayed at temptations, desolations, aridities, faults, in a word, at everything that gives them the impression they are falling lower. They would wish to ascend because they desire to arrive at the summit, because they burn to be united with God; therefore in perceiving that they are apparently descending under the impact of temptations, the weight of their faults, and the void in their souls caused by desolations, they grow confused and grieve because they forget the divine paradoxes of the spiritual life.

Fortunately God does not always heed our protests and our cries of anguish. Instead He pours out upon us those precious graces, even though they may be bitter, which involve temptations, aridities, and even faults, as a mother, despite the wailing and the protests of her child, firmly applies the painful remedy that will give him health.

Some day we shall understand that among the greatest graces God has given us in our life are precisely those disconcerting ones which make us think that God is abandoning us, when on the contrary He is attracting us, and which cause us to judge that we are falling away from our ideal, when on the contrary we are drawing nearer to the sweet goal of our hopes.

O souls eager for perfection, do not weary of

humbling yourselves; have no fear of whatever plunges you into the depth of your misery! We do not depart from God by lowering ourselves; we do so only by exalting ourselves. "Reach up to Him, and He flees from you; lower yourself before Him, and He comes down to you." Do not forget this: if we raise ourselves upward, God flees from us; if we humble ourselves, He comes down to us.

It seems to me that God in His own way feels the dizziness of the abyss: our miserableness, when it is acknowledged and accepted by us, exerts an irresistible attraction on Him. What, save misery alone, can attract mercy? What, save emptiness, can appeal to plenitude? Whither shall the infinite ocean of Goodness pour itself except into the immense abyss of our nothingness?

"I will speak to my Lord, whereas I am dust and ashes." [5] These words of Abraham, "whereas I am dust and ashes," ring in my ears as the cause and the reason of the daring of the Patriarch: "I will speak to my Lord, whereas I am dust and ashes." Behold the one and only reason, powerful and all-embracing, to be sure, that we can adduce before God to speak to Him, to petition Him, in order to press Him for the fulfillment of our most daring desires. And that foundation possesses something of the infinite, seeing that it embraces, as it were, even infinity. I am dust and ashes; for that reason I place no bounds in my petition for mercy; for that reason

[5] Gen. 18:27.

I have confidence; for that reason I have hope; for that reason I dare to ask the Lord even for "the kiss of His mouth," as the spouse in the Canticle of Canticles.

When shall we be convinced that our miserableness makes us "strong against God"? [6] When shall we take cognizance of the fact that to plunge ourselves into our nothingness is the assured means to attract God?

When in our eagerness for God we desire to possess Him, let us not urge our purity or our virtues or our merits to oblige Him to come to our hearts; for either we do not have these things, or we have received them from Him. Let us show Him what is properly our own, the unspeakable misery of our being; let us lower ourselves deeper into the depths of our nothingness. Then the Lord will feel the dizziness caused by the abyss, and He will plunge Himself into the limitless void with the impetuous force of His mercy and His goodness.

We must not think that this secret for drawing down God is the unique property of the beginnings of the spiritual life; no, it applies to all of it. Thanks be to God, our misery has no limits, and thus it can never exhaust infinite mercy.

On the peak of a unique perfection stood the Immaculate Virgin Mary, and in her inspired canticle she attributes the marvels that the Omnipotent effected in her to a glance that the Lord gave. Do

[6] Gen. 32:28.

we know at what? It was her humility. "Because He hath regarded the humility of His handmaid." [7]

The mystery of the union of God with the soul takes place in the depths of the abyss, in the mutual self-abasement of God and the creature.

"Love must always be humble," says Louise Margaret Claret de la Touche.[8] She is right. Love is by nature humble; humility is one of its innate characteristics. For love is forgetful of self; it is a bowing down before the Beloved. And when there is question of divine love which takes place between nothingness and the All, it is utter self-abasement, it is adoration.

God Himself abased Himself in order to love us; He "emptied Himself," as St. Paul says.[9]

And the soul that perceives in its inmost being the deep and intoxicating wound of love also empties itself; and in the abyss of this mutual self-abasement the loving mystery of union is consummated.

The humility of this union is indeed a new kind of humility; it is something completely heavenly, something profound, most sweet, delicious; it is something that only he who has experienced it can know. In the splendor of the light with which God bathes the soul that He approaches, it comprehends its misery in a new way, just as the feeble flame of a little lamp would appear to be darkness

[7] Luke 1:48.
[8] *Les vouloirs de Dieu,* p. 224.
[9] Phil. 2:7.

should the light of the sun engulf it. A soul seeing itself revealed in this light would wish to hide itself, yea, to annihilate itself; but this hiding with its Beloved, this self-abasement, would be that He alone might shine. And such is the anxiety that it feels to abase itself, and so great is the joy that it experiences in its littleness, that if it were anything, even though something great, it would consume itself entirely in a holocaust of love to God, and it would lose itself in the loving self-effacement involved in adoration.

And each new union is a new and deeper self-effacement. Then the soul takes joy in seeing before its eyes an immense abyss into which it can descend, for it knows from sweet experience that each degree of self-abasement is a more intimate embrace with the Beloved; and when once wounded with love, it desires the "kiss of His mouth." Now it no longer beseeches with words that are impotent to express the ardor of its longing; instead it lowers itself into the abyss in order to force the Beloved to come to seek it in the depths and to regale it with the sweetness of His ineffable caresses.

But humility does not attain its perfection until the soul becomes transformed into Jesus; then humility is no longer that timid thing which labors painfully with human miseries in the first stages of the spiritual life, nor is it even the heavenly self-surrender of union. In transformed souls humility is the very humility of Jesus, which is reflected in them; it is the divine thirst for self-effacement that burned in our Lord's innermost being, that burns in the interior of a soul by a participation of love; it is that divine highroad which the Word of God took when, as a giant, He joyously began to run the pathway of love, and came down upon earth skipping over the mountains. And in that roadway He carries with Him the souls that also run after Him, attracted by the sweetness of His perfumes.

What was this delightful roadway but a swift and headlong descent into the abyss of self-efface-ment? "Do you wish to know, dearly beloved," says St. Gregory the Great, "the leaps that He made? He came from heaven into the womb of the Virgin; from this immaculate womb He went to the crib; from the crib He went to the cross; from the cross He went to the tomb." [10] The holy doctor failed to mention the final leap which perpetuates all the rest, namely, that to the Eucharist. And I say that this excels the others, for as St. Thomas sings:

> "In cruce latebat sola deitas
> At hic latet simul et humanitas."

"On the cross only His divinity lay concealed, but here [in the Eucharist] His humanity is also hid-den."

Hence if Jesus is ever descending, why should

[10] *Homilia 29 in Evang.*

we wish to ascend? The soul that is transformed into Him wishes to share His lot, to go where He goes and to abase itself whither He has abased Himself; and inflamed with the divine madness of Jesus, it possesses an insatiable desire of self-effacement. It becomes little with Jesus in the crib, and it offers itself as a victim on Calvary; it wishes like Jesus to be a living host and to disappear from view and to treasure its hidden God under the veil of its misery.

But in the depth of that mystical effacement, which is the spiritual life, in the distinct stages of that glorious descent, the soul ever rises. This it does because, first of all, it approaches God, then it becomes united to Him, and finally it becomes transformed into Him forever; and God is the highest, He is the supreme summit, He is the one and only Most High.

The secret of perfection, then, consists in that divine paradox, "one ascends by descending," and the soul that understands it and never tires of descending finds rest and happiness in the heart of God, in accordance with the profound thought of St. John of the Cross: "In order to come to be all, desire in all things to be nothing."

III

Disorderly Affections

Whenever the affections of the heart are not an expansion of divine love, they are an obstacle to our perfect union with God.

Every affection, to be sure, is not an obstacle; for when divine love takes possession of a soul, it enriches the soul with most pure loves, and these, since they spring from the sturdy trunk of the love of God, are far from being an obstacle; they are, rather, a powerful help to the most intimate union, to perfect holiness, since they are expansions of divine love.

From its inception the love of God demands of us that we love our neighbor, that is to say, all men, good and bad, friends and enemies. And in the exuberance of charity the saints come to love not only the neighbor, whom they are obliged to love, but even inanimate creatures. St. Francis of Assisi is a magnificent example of this spiritual exuberance of love, for his heart embraced with the immense sweep of love not only men, but also all creation: the sun, the water, the fishes, the birds, and even the wolf.

But if every affection that blossoms from the love of God is holy, and if it increases our perfection rather than impedes it, the same is not true of any other affection that has purely human and natural roots; for from affections of this kind come forth sins, both mortal and venial. Inordinate affections are the root of sin.

Judas bore in his heart an inordinate affection for money. I do not know whether this inclination led him into any sin before the Passion. Let us suppose that it did not; nevertheless in his heart stood rooted that evil affection which came to the surface whenever circumstances gave it free play, leading slowly to the consummation of its destructive work. When Magdalen poured out the precious ointment of spikenard upon our Lord's head, Judas became scandalized, and under the appearance of a feigned charity he manifested his disorderly affection: "Why was not this ointment sold for three hundred pence and given to the poor?" But one day that affection burst into the open, and then it was the cause of one of the greatest crimes that has ever defaced the earth, since Jesus said of its perpetrator: "It were better for him if that man had not been born."

When at any time an affection rises to the point of taking complete possession of our heart in such a way that it causes us to place our happiness and our final end in a creature, then mortal sin is committed; for mortal sin is nothing else but the triumph of an inordinate affection over the love of God.

Very often a disorderly affection does not go to such an extreme, yet it can contrive to live side by side with the love of God. Then it is a species of parasite which prevents the love of God from developing in all its fullness and in all its glory. In this case a disorderly affection is the cause only of venial sins or simply of imperfections; yet in every instance it hampers the perfect development of the love of God.

The Gospel also gives us an example of this truth. Before the descent of the Holy Ghost on the apostles, they cherished disorderly affections in their hearts, some, of course, more than others. They thought that the kingdom of Jesus Christ was to be a temporal kingdom, that the Messias was to come to conquer the world and to subject it to the yoke of Israel, and that Christ was to be a conqueror after the manner of Alexander or Caesar; and they desired to occupy various posts in this kingdom. These desires did not carry them to the extent of committing treachery or treason; but they did deprive them of the fervor, devotion, and holy ardor that they should have had on the night of the institution of the Eucharist. For while Jesus was consummating the most stupendous mystery that the ages have ever seen, right there in the Cenacle itself, close to Jesus transfigured, the apostles were disputing about which of them would be the greatest in the kingdom of heaven.

Thus it is with disorderly affections: when they do not go so far as to burst their bonds and produce the supreme tragedy of mortal sin in the soul, they cause venial sins; they are the seed-plot of imperfections, or at least they hinder the perfect development of love in our hearts. They are parasites.

We all know what happens to a plant when it is infested with parasites: it loses its exuberant growth and vigor; it no longer produces flowers or fruits, or it produces such as are diseased and miserable. When a good gardener sees a sickly plant, he at once comes to this conclusion: this plant has parasites; they may be at the roots, or in the stalk, or on the leaves; but have them it does. Similarly, when a soul does not advance in perfection as it should, when it stands, as it were, stock still, even though it does not commit mortal sins, nor even many venial ones, any director of souls can make this judgment: Here are parasites, here are disorderly affections. I do not know what they are, but I do know that they exist, and their presence is what impedes the progress of this soul.

It was for this reason that our Lord taught us in so clear and so precise a manner that, if we are to achieve perfection, an absolute renunciation of all things of this world is necessary; we must root out from our hearts everything that is not the love of

God or that does not have its origin in this love.
This is the truth He set as the foundation of His
doctrine in His sermon on the beatitudes: "Blessed
are the poor in spirit: for theirs is the kingdom of
heaven." The kingdom of heaven is union with
God; it is all-consuming love; it is full participation
in the life of God. And the kingdom of God is for
the poor, for the self-renounced, for those who
have sold all that they possessed, for those who
find themselves in the holy and divine nakedness
of poverty and of love.

There is another passage in the Gospel wherein
our Lord teaches us the same doctrine even more
clearly. "Which of you," says the Master, "having
a mind to build a tower, doth not first sit down and
reckon the charges that are necessary, whether he
have wherewithal to finish it; lest, after he hath laid
the foundation and is not able to finish it, all that
see it begin to mock him saying: 'This man began
to build, and was not able to finish.' Or what king,
about to make war against another king, doth not
first sit down and think whether he be able with
ten thousand men to meet him that with twenty
thousand cometh against him? Or else, whilst the
other is yet afar off, sending an embassy, he de-
sireth conditions of peace. So likewise every one
of you that doth not renounce all that he posses-
seth cannot be My disciple."

At first sight the conclusion seems illogical; for
we do not quite see what connection the king and

the tower have with the renunciation of all that we possess. But if we reflect carefully on this precious teaching of our Lord, we come to understand His meaning. As one needs money to build and soldiers to wage war, so one needs renunciation to achieve perfection. He who has no money should not build, and he who has no soldiers should not wage war; likewise he who will not renounce himself, let him not try to attain perfection; rather let him seek some other employment to which to devote himself.

For it is impossible to achieve perfection without renouncing our possessions, without freeing our hearts of them. God will not take full possession of our hearts until everything else has been expelled. As long as the root of the last disorderly affection that abides in us is not extirpated, the love of God cannot reign with full sovereignty.

And let it be well noted that I do not say the love of God cannot coexist with disorderly affections. They can live side by side, since mortal sin alone destroys the love of God. Neither do I affirm that no one can possess God unless his heart is free from every created thing. Certainly a person can possess God while he is attached to other things; but he cannot possess Him completely. In such a soul our Lord will hold the principal place, the place of honor; but He does not have complete possession nor is He the sole master of that abode. That soul is similar—pardon me the comparison—to a guest-house. Here abides one disorderly affection, there another. God of course dwells in the principal part of the house, and He has a certain dominion over it, but not an absolute dominion; for He is not able to do whatsoever He wishes since the inopportune guests impede His absolute rule.

For this reason our Savior said to the youth in the Gospel: "If thou wilt be perfect, go sell what thou hast, and give to the poor . . . and come follow Me."

The best proof of the importance of this teaching is the way the young man acted. He must have been a pure and holy soul, since he ingenuously says—and our Lord does not contradict him—that he has kept the commandments of God from his youth. Nevertheless, in spite of his eagerness to know the secrets of eternal life and what must be done to obtain it; in spite of the glance of love and predilection from Jesus, the young man departed from Him sorrowfully. The Gospel gives us the reason: it was because he was rich, because he harbored an inordinate affection in his heart. Nor was this a sinful affection. His money was not ill-gotten; neither did he make bad use of it, seeing that he kept the commandments. He simply was unwilling to renounce this created thing to follow Jesus.

How many souls are there in which the scene enacted on the shores of Tiberias is reproduced! These are souls that Jesus calls, upon whom He gazes with love, to whom He offers spiritual riches.

But they depart sadly from Jesus because they hold in their heart the riches of worldly affection which they do not wish to renounce.

The teaching that I have just explained is the teaching of the Gospel; but surely, if we look at it through the divine prism of the heart of Jesus, we shall see it with greater clearness.

How do we see this doctrine of renunciation from the heart of Jesus? To understand it, we must not forget that we do not enter into the heart of Jesus except through love. Love it is that guides us through the mysteries of that heavenly abode; and love it is that reveals to us the riches of that heart; and love it is that causes us to lift ourselves up to the tower that crowns that admirable palace.

And this truth is easy to understand, since through love alone can entrance be gained into any heart; no other way can be found for entering hearts. Let no one say that some hearts open up to money, for it is not true. Money conquers all, except the heart. For the sake of money, man can be changed into a slave and stoop to deeds of lowest baseness; but he does not surrender his heart. This has only one key: love. It is by love we enter into any heart, divine or human. Hence everything that is an obstacle to love is an obstacle to entering in and living in the heart of Jesus.

Now indeed it can be stated that the only obstacle to love is some other love; for love is exclusive; it will not tolerate anything else in its own sphere. Love goes everywhere; but it will never go where the beloved heart is divided; it will never deign to share this heart with others. Love is like that.

We see this most clearly in our Lord. He comes down to our lowliness; He overlooks all our defects, for no one is so indulgent and merciful as He. They who do not know God think that He is most demanding, that He has, as it were, a microscope by which to discover our faults, and that He will not allow a single one to get by Him, no matter how slight it may be. It is true that by reason of His holiness and His justice He, in a certain sense, does not allow any fault to escape Him, for justice demands that every failing be either atoned for or punished. But we must not forget that His mercy and His love are equally infinite with His justice and His holiness, and, consequently, that there is no one so ready to condescend, to pardon, and to bear with us as Jesus is.

May He be blessed because He is such! If He were not as He is, what would become of us? Most truly a God of infinite mercy and love is necessary to support us, since we are all too weak to support one another; we cannot even support ourselves. But our Lord is indeed infinitely merciful and indulgent, and He bears with us. It appears that we are made for one another: an infinite God, unbounded in love and in mercy, for such a miserable creature as man! Does not this make us understand well?

But one thing He will not overlook, because He cannot tolerate it, namely, a divided love. He does not wish our heart to be shared between God and creatures, because He wishes our whole heart.

One would say that He is satisfied with the heart. It is true that besides the heart we must give Him all our strength and all our will, because He Himself has said so: "Thou shalt love the Lord thy God with thy whole heart and with thy whole soul and with thy whole mind." But with the exception of the heart, He seems to admit delays in all things else, and to bear Himself indulgently. Should there be failings in our exterior life, should we have certain faults of character, should we not give Him the full fruits of our garden—no matter. Our Lord waits, He bears with our weaknesses. But what He will not compound with is our heart: He wishes it in its entirety.

And He wishes it completely because He loves us, because love is like that: the desire for complete possession is its essential characteristic.

For this reason our Lord battles unremittingly and at times cruelly—at least so it appears to us— against the inordinate affections of our heart. He is even capable of allowing us to fall into sin in order to cure us of some hidden affection in our heart.

How many times, for instance, in the case of proud souls that are enamored of themselves and that consequently deny Him the pledged homage of their love, He lets them fall into sin, when there is no other way whereby to arouse them to a holy humility, yes, and even into mortal sin!

What awe-inspiring mystery! To think that our Lord would tolerate such a catastrophe in order to save that poor soul; so that, after having sunk into the mire, it would rise and understand its misery, and then cast away the little idol that it was cherishing in its heart and at length give itself to Him without reserve! This was so with Mary Magdalen, St. Augustine, and many others. It is an occurrence that we see frequently in the world of the spirit.

What are these interior pains, which at times are so piercing, if not the war of our Lord against disorderly affections? Souls secretly harbor, at times even unknowingly, certain microscopic parasites. By itself a soul would never be aware of their presence or be able to get rid of them; and yet those parasites stand in the way of our Lord, because everything, no matter how small, that opposes love, opposes Him.

Hence comes cruel and agonizing desolation in order to rid the heart of these parasites. The soul weeps, it feels moved to despair, it cries to the Lord from the abyss of its misery; but God seems deaf, and He continues His work almost heartlessly, so that apparently the tears and cries of the soul do not move Him.

Does He no longer have a heart of mercy? On the contrary, He loves greatly. Moved by love He withdraws Himself, in order to purify that soul, to rid it of those microscopic parasites by means of pain and sorrow, so that love may blossom and fructify in that soul of His choice.

Considered from the heart of Jesus, disorderly affections are enemies of love. Each of them robs Jesus of a fiber of our heart. And He desires that we love Him with our whole heart. In fact, this demand of our Lord is most just. For how could we reasonably share it, seeing that it is so poor and so small?

But what has been said applies not only to divine love, as was mentioned above. All love is alike: it demands the whole heart. Not even the basest creature is content with a portion of the heart; much less, then, can God be thus satisfied. And can we bring ourselves to give only a part of our heart to God, even though the largest and the best part? Is it not true that we wish to give our whole heart to our Lord, and have we not assured Him many times that it does belong entirely to Him?

Every Christian is bound by many titles to give his whole heart to God: because He is our Creator from whom we have received everything; because He is our Redeeemer who has purchased us with His blood; because to deprive Jesus of a single strand of our heart is robbery, since it is His, since He has bought it, and at a most dear price. How then can we deprive Him of a single fiber of that heart?

But souls that are consecrated to God—in the priesthood and in the religious life—have many special reasons that oblige them more than the simple faithful to give their whole heart to God: because we have chosen Him with complete freedom of soul for our only inheritance, for our only possession: "The Lord is the portion of my inheritance"; because we have freely and solemnly given Him our whole heart. Is not this fundamentally the essence of the religious profession? The religious promises are apparently only poverty, chastity, and obedience; but at the base of these three things lies love. Our Lord would not be satisfied with our oblation if it should lack as its basis the great, supreme oblation, that is, the gift of ourselves, the offering of our heart.

In addition to our religious profession, how many times in our life have we told God that our heart belongs to Him without reserve! Our offerings were sincere, and God accepted them as such. Perhaps we have not realized sufficiently that the least disorderly affection that exists in us is a theft; that by it we deprive Jesus of love; that by it we snatch away a portion of our heart from Him to retain it for ourselves or to give it to the creature that we have set up within us.

If we love, let us render our whole heart. Let us not concern ourselves too much about our frailties and our failings; nobody knows better than Jesus the clay from which we are formed; nobody knows better than He how to commiserate our weakness and how to condescend to our frailty. But there is one thing about which we should concern ourselves: our heart. Let it be pure, let it be free of all attachments, let it be solely for Jesus. Let us not hold out for the least fragment of our heart; let us not take the minutest particle for ourselves: all must be for Jesus.

Some souls do not understand why or how affections can be an obstacle to perfection. They think that only those inclinations that tend to sin must be eradicated. This is how they reason: against which of God's commandments does this affection which I have in my heart fail? Against what precept does it sin? It is not against any. Therefore there can be no evil in it.

Let us grant that there is nothing present that can actually be called sin. Nevertheless that affection is depriving our Lord of a portion of our heart; it is robbing Him of a share in our affection; and on this point God is most jealous.

Nor does it matter that this thing is small, that we hardly attach any importance to it; for little things can develop into great effects. What are smaller than microbes? Yet they are the cause of sicknesses and even of death. How many times do the parasites, which we can hardly see, ruin plants and render them fruitless! And in a machine of great precision even a slight speck of dust can mar its operation. Similarly those affections that appear insignificant do, nevertheless, impede the work of our sanctification.

Have we not felt from time to time that some barrier stands between Jesus and our heart? We love Him, and He loves us: there can be no doubt of this. He draws near to our souls, He unites Himself to them, and He caresses them tenderly; and we also love Him. Still, in some indefinable way, we feel a barrier, some hindrance which prevents us from uniting ourselves completely with Him. What can it be? The hindrances that prevent Jesus from uniting Himself to our souls are our disorderly affections. The moment we are entirely free of them our heart will expand and cast itself completely into the heart of Jesus; then He will give Himself to us without reserve. Is it right for us to keep retarding the consummation of our love and our union with Jesus because of some trifling affections that really do not amount to anything?

No worldly love is worth anything, for it possesses only an apparent value. Because he was rich, the youth in the Gospel was unwilling to follow Jesus. What foolishness! Yet grant that his riches do mean something from a human point of view. One might understand how a person might not wish to follow Jesus because he had a fortune of several million dollars and was unwilling to renounce it. But how can one understand not wishing to follow Him because of an attachment to a few pennies? Yet fundamentally both cases are equally foolish; for, seen through the eyes of faith, no difference exists between a few pennies and many millions of dollars. Yes, even from a human point of view it is sheer foolishness not to give our whole heart to our Lord because of some trifle. And let us remark this well: frequently the things that keep us from going to God are trifles, poor little attachments that are not worth bothering with.

Consequently it is indispensable that we root out every inordinate affection from our heart, because each one opposes love, hinders our perfect union with God, and gradually renders our soul fruitless. Let us then enter into our heart; let us see if there is any bagatelle there that is impeding our Lord from having full sway over us; and let us root it out ruthlessly.

If we do not discover anything, or if we are not able to pluck it out, let us say to our Lord: "I must have some parasite in my heart, O Lord; I do not know where it is, nor am I able to free myself of it. But I place myself in Thy hands. Come, O Lord, with Thy scalpel, or with Thy fire, or with whatever thing Thou dost wish, to rid me of it; purify my heart and dispose it for complete union with Thyself."

Then, when these parasites have disappeared

from our heart, we shall see how a new love springs up within us. Jesus will give Himself to us without any reserve. Free of restraints and hindrances, these two hearts, Jesus' and our own, will merge; and they will become one in the ineffable mystery of love.

IV

Confidence Despite All

▲▲

It is not rare in the spiritual life to see souls that try generously to advance in virtue fall, by reason of their desire to cultivate a delicate conscience and to avoid all deliberate venial sin, into the extremity of inquietude and perturbation, get involved in a thousand perplexities and scruples, and eventually grow cold in their trust in our Lord. All these occurrences spell the death of devotion.

The following short reflections are given to help avoid this dangerous shoal. Hence I do not tire of repeating to all generous souls: be as delicate as you can with our Lord; watch your conduct most carefully to avoid all venial sins; but, for the love of God, let this be done without losing confidence and peace.

This recommendation I exalt to such a degree that, were it necessary to lose these two goods, confidence and peace, in order to arrive at this exquisite delicacy, I maintain that it would be preferable to restrain one's efforts for a while; for peace of soul and confidence in God are more necessary goods and, consequently, they should be preferred.

Nor are they to be preferred only so far as they pertain to ourselves, that is, in saving us pains, for no generous soul ought ever to refuse any sacrifice; but they are to be preferred in the very interest of our Lord. For, with the very holy and very rightful aim of sparing our Lord the slight wound that a venial sin causes him, one deprives Him of the great satisfaction and pleasure He experiences in the progress of a soul in its sanctification when it trusts in Him and lives at peace.

Let us give an example that we may explain our meaning better. A fervent soul has the misfortune to commit a venial sin, an occurrence which is not rare considering our innate frailty. Just as soon as this soul has fallen, it recalls everything that it has read and reflected on concerning venial sin, and forthwith it becomes disturbed, overwhelmed with sorrow and suffering. Confidence in God grows cold; the soul withdraws from Him; it leaves off prayer, or makes it badly; all its exercises of piety no longer are made with their customary regularity. After many hours of inquietude it recovers peace of mind, but only by dint of much effort and many consultations. Is it not true that our Lord has lost more during all these hours of perturbation than He has gained? For the soul deprived Him of the joy that it could have given Him in its prayer and in its acts of worship; it failed in trust in Him, a thing which saddens His divine heart; and it lost time by impeding the advancement of its sanctification.

Let us not act in this manner; rather, let us consider how we can perfectly reconcile the grief caused by our sins with confidence in God and peace of soul.

St. Theresa of the Child Jesus expresses this reconciliation very well when she says: "This I know very well: although I should have on my soul all the crimes that could be committed, I would lose none of my confidence; rather, I would hasten, with my heart broken into pieces by sorrow, to cast myself into the arms of my Savior. I know how greatly He loved the prodigal son; I have marked His words to Mary Magdalen, to the adulterous woman, to the Samaritan. No, no one could make me afraid, because I know to whom to cling by reason of His love and His mercy. I know that all this multitude of offenses would disappear in the twinkling of an eye, as a drop of water cast into a roaring furnace."

Let us note this well: a heart broken into pieces by sorrow, and yet undiminished confidence. These two go together in such a way that, although St. Theresa might have been laden with all the sins of the world, she would have flung herself into the arms of Jesus with complete confidence.

No doubt someone will say: How is it possible to feel that keen grief for one's offense against God, and yet have the confidence necessary to cast oneself, without any misgivings, without any reserve, into the arms of our Lord? I am going to attempt an explanation.

The foundation of our confidence does not rest in us, but in God. Hence we trust in our Lord and we draw near to Him, tranquil and sure, not because of what we are, but because of what He is. We can be ingrates, wretches, criminals; still our ingratitude, our wickedness, and our crimes should not diminish by one jot the trust that we should have in our Lord, for the simple reason that our trust is based, not in ourselves, but in Him; and Jesus is the same forever, ever good, ever loving, ever merciful. I was the one who changed, but these changes in no wise affect my confidence, since my confidence is based on God, not on myself.

Let us give an example. Suppose, gentle reader, that you have deposited in the bank a large sum of money upon which you can draw at will. One day you grow ill of a grave and serious sickness. In this condition you are asked to sign a check for less than the amount of money you have on deposit. But you object: "How can I sign the check when I am ill." Now your illness in no way affects your credit at the bank; it affects only your health, not your deposit, which remains intact. "That is true," you say, "but I am ill." Your illness has nothing to do with the matter. If you no longer had any money in the bank, you would not be able to draw on it;

but since your deposit remains intact, you are able to draw on it even though you are ill.

A soul that falls and loses confidence reasons with the same lack of logic. "How can I with full confidence draw near to God if I am an ingrate, if I am loaded down with sins?" Let us see. Do you have resources in the bank? Yes, for therein is the goodness of God, which is infinite; therein is His love, which has suffered no diminution; therein is His mercy, which is unbounded. What does it matter, then, that you are what you are, as long as God, despite your miseries, continues to be what He is?

It will be objected, of course, that the comparison is not exact, since sickness has no relationship with bank deposits, whereas our sins and our ingratitude cannot help but have a relationship with confidence in God. Nevertheless I affirm that there is no relationship. Do we confide in God because of our virtues? Or because we have no sins? If this were the case, then, without doubt, we would not be able to confide in Him whenever we should have fallen into sin. But that is not the truth of the matter. We confide in God because of His goodness, His mercy, and His love. And does God cease to be good and merciful because I am weak, inconstant, and miserable? Impossible.

This is what is happening. We are trying to judge of God in a human manner; we would measure His divine heart with the yardstick of our petty heart;

and it is not God's yardstick. We, of course, conduct ourselves with everyone according to his merits: we are good toward those who treat us well; we are indifferent toward strangers; and only virtue can keep us from being hostile toward our enemies. In order that our heart may love, it must always take into account that which resides in others, for our love has its basis in the things that we love: in the goodness that they possess, or seem to possess. But this basis is not true with God. The measure and the reason of His love does not reside in things or in us; they are in Him and in Him alone.

The theologians say that God's being is *a se*, that is, self-existing Being. He is not like us, who have received being from someone else. The reason of the being of created things is not in themselves; it is outside of themselves: in the causes that produced them, and ultimately in the First Cause, which is God. The reason of God's being, on the contrary, is not outside Himself, but in Himself. And as is His being, so is His love. God loves because He is love, because He is love *a se*, a love that does not depend on anyone. Consequently the fact that I may be better or worse, more ungrateful or more grateful, has nothing at all to do with the basis of my confidence.

May God deliver us from confiding in ourselves! May God deliver us from lacking trust in Him because of our deficiency! If we are laggards or ingrates or sinners, we shall do very well to mistrust ourselves. But why go to the extent of lacking confidence in God? What relationship have our sins and our ingratitudes with the goodness, the mercy, the love of God? All His attributes are infinite, and they have no absolute relationship with any created thing.

Hence the only thing that could shake our confidence would be to come to the knowledge that God is no longer so good and so merciful as hitherto; but as long as this does not occur—and it will never occur—we must confide completely in Him.

Furthermore, I dare to say that if we should have this knowledge by means of a private revelation, we must not believe it. If an angel from heaven should come to say to us, "God no longer loves you; hence you must no longer confide in Him," do not believe him. Rather, we could say to him, "You are not a messenger of God, but an envoy of the devil," since a messenger of God does not speak in this manner.

In treating of hope, St. Thomas Aquinas says something in this vein. After explaining that the virtue of hope gives us the holy assurance of our salvation, he proposes this objection to himself: If someone has a revelation that he is going to be damned, what should he do? Nothing more than not believe it, replies the holy doctor; for that revelation is contrary to the virtue of hope, and therefore it cannot come from God.

In like manner I maintain that if an angel should come from God to tell anyone of us, "God no longer loves you; hence do not confide in Him," we must not believe him; for above this feigned revelation stands the word of Jesus, "Heaven and earth shall pass away, but My word shall not pass away." Jesus is the one who brought us a message from heaven. He came to tell us that God loves us with an infinite love, with an eternal love; that He loves us to the extent of having given us His own Son, and having delivered Him to death for love of us.

Now, no doubt, I shall be objected to with this question: Is there never, then, a moment when God ceases to love us? There is only one. Should we have the misfortune to die impenitent, He would cease loving us in the last moment of our life. Only final impenitence, the consummation of our misfortune, can separate us from the love of God. Before this moment, the last of our life, the love of God does not fail. In spite of everything, He always loves us. Hence as long as this moment does not come, we must believe in the love, in the goodness, and in the mercy of God toward us; and on this most solid foundation we must base our hope.

Now, if the foundation of our hope does not become shattered because we may have had the misfortune to commit all possible crimes, how can it be shaken because we have committed a venial sin? This trust in God does not prevent sin from making us feel sorrowful; for all sin, grave or light, large or small, wounds His divine heart, and, since we love Him, naturally we should feel great sorrow for having offended Him. Thus we have as our portion sorrow on one side, and confidence on the other: we must cast ourselves into the arms of our Savior with our heart torn to pieces by contrition, as St. Theresa of the Child Jesus says.

Thus confidence and contrition are not incompatible; on the contrary, both flow from the same fount, love. I feel pain at having offended God, because I love Him; I confide in Him because He loves me, because, as says the saint of Lisieux, "I know to whom to cling by reason of the love and the mercy of Jesus."

But the objections are not yet exhausted; hence this point can be made: When I have offended our Lord, when I have wounded His sacred heart, does He love me just the same as before? Indubitably. And I even make so bold as to say, using our human mode of speaking, that He loves us more than before, because our Lord is most generous.

When a child commits a fault against his mother, there is no doubt that she feels it and is hurt by it. But does the mother cease to love her child because of it? Nor does a mother have to be heroic and exceptional to keep loving the child that has afflicted her, for every mother knows how to do this. Nor is this all; for one of the very qualities of motherly tenderness is this, that the pain caused by the ingratitude of her child arouses, in a certain sense, her tenderness and her love; and thus if it cannot be said that she loves him more, at least one can be sure that she will exert herself more in showing her love for him in order to attract him to her motherly embrace and to secure his correction and reform. And shall a mother be more generous than our Lord?

I think that all our mistrust in God would be a true injury to Him, something that would wound Him excessively, if it were not the result of our ignorance. This is the same as saying that our Lord pardons the offense we commit against Him in mistrusting Him for the same reason that He sought pardon for His executioners: "Because they know not what they do."

But in reality that mistrust is something very injurious to our Lord. Is not to lack trust in God, judging His heart to be like ours—circumscribed and paltry, narrow and base, changeable and peevishly inconstant?

The first thing that many souls do, as soon as they have had the misfortune to commit an offense, is to withdraw from our Lord. What a strange thing! They withdraw from our Lord, and when do they plan to return to Him? Perhaps after their confession. But how can one make a confession without drawing near to Jesus? Who washes them? Who cleanses them? No doubt they will say to me that our Lord does so, but through the medium of His minister; and, they will add, it is less difficult for them to go to him. This is the same thing as one person, who is offended at another, but from whom he needs a favor, not daring to ask it directly, but employing an intermediary. What an aberration! How is it possible to have more trust in the priest, no matter how holy he may be, than in Jesus Himself?

Thus if He is the only one who can cleanse us, if He is the only one who can pardon us, to whom shall we have recourse but to Him? Consequently, whenever we may have the misfortune to commit an offense, no matter what kind, venial or mortal, even a crime to which an excommunication is attached, the first thing that we should do is to cast ourselves into the arms of our Lord, filled with grief, but also filled with confidence. How much time souls lose in their act of withdrawing from our Lord when they have committed an offense! Why do they delay? If the only one who can cleanse them is Jesus . . . !

This course is also to judge our Lord in a very human manner. When we have offended a man, our delay is justified; for it is very natural for his passion to become aroused when he sees himself offended, and hence we must wait until his ire passes and his soul calms down. But since our Lord is always calm, why do we delay? At length we shall come to cast ourselves in His arms, since there is no hope nor peace nor pardon nor anything in anyone else. Hence the sooner the better, for He ever holds His arms outstretched to us.

What I have just said is not a new doctrine contrived by St. Theresa of the Child Jesus; much less is it a teaching of the twentieth century. It is as old as the Gospel. There our Lord teaches it in an insistent and clear manner. What happens is this: either we do not read the Gospel, or we do not take it seriously.

Let us take, for example, the parable of the prodigal son. That youth did not commit light offenses, but very grave sins; he left his father's house; he demanded his inheritance in order to waste it in a riotous life. And if now he was returning, it was not so much for love toward his father as need for himself. Not until he sees himself degraded, hungry, and without hope does he decide to return to his father to seek pardon. All during the time this son lived far from him, the father went out to the highway every day to see whether perchance he might see him returning. When one day he sees him, he runs to meet him, embraces him, and does not even give him time to say the words of sorrow that he had prepared.

Who is the father of the prodigal son? Is he not Jesus? Does He not show us His own heart in this parable? Does He not teach us that, when we depart from Him, He goes out to see us, and awaits us; and when He sees us from afar, He runs out to meet us, opens His arms to us, yes, even His very heart, and makes a feast for us?

This parable contains the truth that I made bold to enunciate: as a mother's maternal tenderness is expanded and quickened when her son has offended her, so our Lord loves us more tenderly when we fall and withdraw from Him. Let us recall that the brother of the prodigal son became indignant, and apparently with reason. He said: "I have always loved my father; I have ever remained at his side, and never have I caused him any grief; notwithstanding this, he has never given me a kid to make merry with my friends. And when this one, who has wasted his substance living riotously, returns, a celebration is held." At this point our Lord tells us with full clarity, in order that we may not think this incident has any other explanation, "There shall be joy in heaven upon one sinner that doth penance, more than upon ninety-nine just who need not penance." Does not this show us that in some way our Lord manifests an especial tenderness when a fallen soul repents and returns to His arms?

There is also the parable of the Good Shepherd who goes out to seek the lost sheep, leaving the ninety-nine faithful souls. Over rough paths and through thick brambles the Good Shepherd searches tirelessly. When at length He finds it, He does not scold, nor punish; He takes it gently in His arms, places it on His shoulders, and returns it to the sheepfold. Such is the heart of Jesus.

He teaches us this same truth not only in His parables, but also in His clear and explicit doctrines; for one might yet object that we do not understand His parables well. But there can be no doubt when Christ, our Lord Himself, speaks to us in this explicit manner: "They that are in health need not a physician, but they that are ill. . . . I am not come to call the just, but sinners."

We can arrive at the same conclusion by another road. When we have the misfortune to fall, we certainly commit an act of ingratitude toward Him who loves us so much. But at the same time our misery is brought to light, and we feel, together with our sorrow for having sinned, shame at seeing our misery and our baseness exposed. Yet this misery possesses the mysterious privilege of attracting our Lord. This is difficult to understand, yet it is an incontestable truth. Our nothingness and our misery constitute the force that attracts our Lord.

Oh, foolish people that we are, who believe that it is our natural talents, our good works, and our virtues that attract our Lord; and who, therefore, often wish to parade all this when we present ourselves before Him.[1]

---

[1] The teaching that is given here by the illustrious archbishop is most clear and luminous, and it is far from needing any explanation.

If I may be pardoned the expression, I would say that all this is a species of "spiritual show."

As village maids think that putting on showy ribbons is the way to be elegant and the way to attract attention in society, so souls that suffer from this "spiritual show," and they are legion, wish also to bedeck themselves with showy ribbons and to present themselves before our Lord gaudily attired with their pretended virtues and good points. This is the fault that the Pharisee in the Gospel suffered from when he came before God and standing began to say: "I fast twice in the week, I give tithes, I am not like the rest of men." Spiritual show! We

---

However, as there may be some narrow spirit that might understand it amiss, this clarification is appended.

Whoever would pretend to arrive at this conclusion would commit a grave error: If good works do not attract our Lord, why take the trouble to practice virtues and to perform good deeds? Let it be noted at once and independently of all things else that good works are something strictly obligatory.

On the other hand, good works are more the fruit of grace, that is of God, than of the soul. The soul puts only two things in good works: 1. Everything that is imperfect and deficient in them, by reason of self-love, lack of purity of intention, etc. 2. Correspondence to grace, which is the only good that pertains to us in the practice of virtue. But this cooperation is something very mysterious, since in it grace also plays a great part. Correspondence with grace is in itself a grace.

Despite the little good that there is of ourselves in the practice of virtues and in good works, God accepts them graciously and rewards them, just as a father who gives his son all that he has, yet who graciously accepts the offering that his son makes him out of his own gifts.

In every instance, those good works are posterior to the love and the graces of God. God has given us His grace to do good because He loves us. Hence those works are not the reason why God has descended to our misery; rather our misery and our nothingness are the cause.

already know our Lord's judgment of the Pharisee
and His commendation of the poor publican.

The Most Holy Virgin gives us this same teaching when she says that God did great things in her,
"because He hath regarded the humility of His
handmaid." Perhaps we think that the Blessed
Virgin says this out of humility. There is no doubt
about it whatever; but precisely because she is
humble she speaks the truth. And it is the truth that
even in her our Lord met with that alone which He
cannot help but meet with in all creatures: lowliness and nothingness.

Perhaps we believe that what attracted our Lord
to the Most Holy Virgin was her purity and her
humility. No. Purity, humility, and all the graces
that the Blessed Virgin received were posterior to
the love of God. God first became enamoured of
her, and because He did become enamoured of her,
He enriched her with so many graces. Hence what
He saw in Mary before all these virtues, graces, and
spiritual riches is what He sees in all creation,
which of itself is nothing more than lowliness and
nothingness: "because He hath regarded the humility of His handmaid."

A comparison will make us understand this
teaching better. Let us suppose that a king falls in
love with a peasant maid, and because he is in love
with her he gives her rich clothing and precious
jewels. Who is going to believe that it was the
clothing and the jewels that attracted the king to

the peasant? For these were later gifts of the king; before them there was something else in the peasant that attracted him.

Similarly, the spiritual clothing and jewels in our souls with which He Himself has made us resplendent could not attract our Lord, since all this is a gift of His love. Beforehand, something in us attracted Him; and this can be nothing but that which we alone have of ourselves, our misery and our nothingness. In this way our misery and our nothingness are our titles to be loved. Hence when we present ourselves before God, instead of making a show of our pretended virtues, we must recognize and confess our misery and our nothingness, for they are what attracts God.

This is why I do not tire of repeating that there is an infallible means of attracting our Lord, and—I shall dare to say it—of obtaining from Him whatever we will, namely, our nothingness. A soul that abases itself is all-powerful before God. If we should understand this, how our life would be transformed! And, furthermore, this "spiritual display," which is so common among souls, would be at an end.

Thus whenever we fall or perceive our misery and our nothingness more keenly, then in a certain sense our Lord manifests more tenderness and mercy toward us; for our fall forces us to bring into the light our nothingness and to show forth our misery, and thus God feels more attracted to-

ward us and appears to love us more. Hence if our
Lord loves us in spite of our miseries and even of
our sins, this means that even when we have the
misfortune to fall we must not lose confidence and
peace.

Have I had the ill fortune to sin? I shall repent
at once; I shall break my heart in pieces with sorrow; but I shall not lose my peace, for I know that
our Lord loves me even though I have fallen. I
shall wipe away my sin by contrition; I shall ex-
piate it with penance; but at the same time I shall
cast myself into the arms of Jesus and I shall remain at peace.

Summary and conclusion. Let us be very delicate with our Savior, and the more delicate the
better; let us carefully avoid not only grave faults,
but even all deliberate venial sin. But let us never
lose confidence and peace. Rather let us, with our
heart filled with grief, cast ourselves into the arms
and into the most loving heart of Jesus.

V

Might and Mildness

▀▀

Mighty is the work of sanctification. Over the chaos of our miseries, over the dry and empty waste of our poor heart, is seen the Spirit; and His fruitful breath causes a richer and more beautiful creation to arise than that which sprang forth in the beginning of time from the hands of the Almighty. A holy soul. There is no richness that can equal it, nor any work of art that is comparable to it. It is the delight of God because He sees in it a likeness of His Word, the Son of His eternal joys. And how is this masterpiece produced?

It comes into being as the material world was formed: greatness from above, and baseness from below. From on high is the Spirit that passes over the waters; from below is our soul which receives the divine breath, and which as a docile instrument responds obediently to the action, the will, and the thought of God. Sacred Scripture says that Wisdom "reacheth from end to end mightily and ordereth all things sweetly." In similar fashion is the work of holiness accomplished, for it is a result of might and of mildness.

To sanctify a soul great power is needed; indeed, infinite power. "Who can make him clean, that is conceived of unclean seed? is it not Thou who only art?" [1]

To sanctify souls there was required the force of the wisdom that fashioned the Incarnation, and the might of the sorrow that wrought the mystery of Calvary, and the power of the love, strong as death, which produced the Eucharist.

The action of God in the sanctification of each soul is a marvel of power. What force is necessary to snatch us from sin to which our poor nature is bound with many bonds! What might is in the divine voice that calls us to enter into the land of mystery, the land of vision! What is the power of the love that God allows to fall into our hearts as a spark which kindles and turns into a flame and eventually burns like a volcano! What might is in the cross to which we must nail ourselves with Christ in order to achieve sanctity! All the power of God's all-powerful right hand is needed to make us saints.

On our side holiness is also the effect of power, since only those who exercise force achieve it. That is why there are so few saints. What is sanctity but the deification of our entire being? It is a profound recollection of spirit that concentrates upon God;

[1] Job 14:4.

it is the absolute simplification of the heart that fixes itself positively and firmly upon God; it is the complete transformation of our will that merges and loses itself in the loving will of God; it is the spiritualization of our poor body, to use another term, that in bearing the sufferings of Christ becomes an instrument of the soul, and arrives even to rejoice in God. "My heart and my flesh have rejoiced in the living God." [2]

What prodigies of strength are necessary to fix the inconstancy of the spirit which is ever restless, to hold in check the fickle heart, to rule the rebellious will, and to lift up the base and gross flesh from its connatural slime!

Aloysius Gonzaga striving with indefatigable patience hour after hour to avoid distractions in prayer; Augustine fighting as a giant against past memories and the fierce revolts of the present; Theresa of Jesus polishing for many years with incredible patience the brilliant facets of her heart in order to present it to her Beloved; Hilary bending the body to the spirit with great and heroic mortifications; Ignatius handing himself over to the cruel teeth of wild beasts as the pure white wheat of Christ in order to be changed into spotless bread: these eloquently proclaim to us the enormous power that is necessary for holiness.

Who would find this easy to believe, namely, that mildness is just as necessary as force, perhaps

[2] Ps. 83:3.

even more so, to become a saint? Mildness is not
weakness; rather it is an indication of strength.
Weak souls do their works with noise and show;
the strong operate with marvelous gentleness. Life
is as strong as it is gentle; love is as powerful as it
is delicate; hence the action of God upon nature,
in history, and on souls is infinitely mighty and infinitely mild.

The action of God upon His saints is most gentle.
How He respects our liberty! How He condescends
to our weakness! He does not run, nor jump, nor
act violently. We, being weak creatures, rush; but
God works slowly because He deals with eternity.
We bewail the passage of minutes; but God se-
renely watches the flow of years. We wish to
achieve the goal of our desires with a single rush;
but God prepares His work gently, nor does our
inconstancy weary Him, nor do our failures startle
Him, nor the complicated vicissitudes of human
life overturn His eternal designs.

Conversions are prodigies of gentleness, such as
was St. Augustine's. The long stages necessary for
union are prodigies of gentleness, such paths as St.
Theresa traveled. Great missions from God are also
prodigies of gentleness, such as was St. Margaret
Mary Alacoque's. If we knew how to study the divine action in every saint, in every soul, we would
be astonished, perhaps more at the gentleness than
at the power of the sanctifying action.

Gentleness is indispensable for us if we are to

become holy; and this we frequently forget. Undoubtedly many souls do not sanctify themselves because of a lack of power; but many also, indeed very many, fail to do so because of a want of gentleness.

The human soul is precious and delicate. It came forth from the divine lips as a most gentle breath; it is cleansed and rendered beautiful with the divine blood of Jesus; and it is destined to be united with God Himself to participate in the life and in the ineffable mystery of the Most Blessed Trinity.

Such an exquisite jewel must be handled with consummate delicacy. That is how God treats it, and that is how we should treat it. What an atmosphere of purity of mind, of peace, and of delicacy ought to surround a soul for it to achieve its sanctification! When the soul is borne to another atmosphere, how it pines, how it laments! It is like those beautiful and delicate flowers which a strong wind withers or the heat of the sun discolors and parches.

I think that the greater part of the spiritual ills of souls that seek perfection comes from a lack of gentleness. Gentleness is needful to these poor, ever disquieted souls. Desirous of holiness, they would achieve it all at once. They cannot countenance their own miseries, they grow angry at their weaknesses, and with an overrefinement of ingenuity they continually worry and grieve themselves.

Unknowing and proud, they have not discovered the secret of mildness, the daughter of love, which is patient and benign. If they possessed this secret, they would understand that one arrives at perfection by paths that are strewn with imperfections, which must be borne with humility; that when a soul falls, it does not arise with agitation, but gently places itself in the merciful hands of God by means of humility and trust in Him; that God does not ask for the perfection of our conduct, but for the perfection of our heart, as the wonderfully mild St. Francis of Sales so admirably teaches us.

Mildness is necessary to these souls who are so strict with themselves, even to the point of excess. They have forgotten the pages of the Gospel wherein we are told about mercy and love; they see in Christ only the severe countenance of Judge, without remembering that He is also Friend, Father, Spouse, and, above all, Savior, who came to heal our miseries. They do not know that the sweet honey of love achieves more with the poor human heart than the bitter gall of severity. It seems that they still live on Sinai, that they have never placed their foot in the Cenacle, and that they have never uttered the consoling and victorious cry of the beloved disciple: "And we have known, and have believed the charity, which God hath to us." [3] They do not believe in love.

Mildness is required in the desolations of spirit

[3] I John 4:16.

of those souls who would free themselves violently, without thinking that in this way they only increase their pain. Gentleness is needful in prayer, for there are souls who become angry at distractions, and who wish at all events to travel by the road that pleases them, whereas they ought to allow themselves to be borne gently by the Spirit, who inclines where He wills, and whose comings in and goings out we do not understand. Gentleness is needful for recollection, seeing that one would try to obtain it with violence, whereas the imagination is restrained and the powers of the soul are brought to concentration only by a delicate gentleness.

Mildness is necessary in order that the soul may know itself, seeing that the very gifts of God are not recognized—shameful ingratitude!—out of a fear of falling into pride, as though humility were not truth itself, according to the happy phrase of St. Theresa. Gentleness is necessary; but why go on? Enough has been said to open these consoling vistas to souls that have need of them.

The soul is a delicate thing: a reflection of God, a breath of the Most High. Let it be treated as it deserves, that, poised on the strong wings of might and of mildness, it may ascend to the holy regions for which it was born, that it may soar up to the bosom of God, who is infinite Might and infinite Mildness.

VI

The Three Stages of Sorrow

One of the most important things in the spiritual life is to understand well the intimate relations between love and sacrifice. That love is the basis of perfection is easily understood, and the soul delights in confirming it; for love marvelously corresponds to something deep that the soul bears in its interior: to a vital yearning that is vehement and in a certain sense unparalleled. And when the soul comes in contact with the ephemeral, the superficial, the emptiness of the affections of earth, it impetuously flings itself toward that divine love which is so profound that it reaches to the deepest part of the soul, into regions that mundane affections never sound. It is so perfect that it satisfies forever without ever wearying, and so enduring that it is immortal, yes, even inamissible, so that nothing and no one can uproot it when it has implanted itself in the heart.

Frequently, however, one has an inexact concept of love; for some dream of a love that is not of this world, that was perhaps the love of the earthly Paradise, that will be undoubtedly the love of heaven: a love that is a perpetual feast, that is unalloyed joy. And when the soul spies the summit of that delightful Thabor, it exclaims, as did St. Peter, without knowing what it says: "It is good for us to be here." It does not understand that in this life to love is to suffer, that the eternal symbol of love on this earth is the cross of Christ, that to arrive at love we must ascend the steep and bloody slopes of Calvary, that to be united with Love we must be nailed with Christ to the cross itself, and that to be suffused with love we must be lowered into the ocean of bitterness which Jesus conceals in His loving heart.

When we come to understand that perfection consists in love, and that this love is attained, conserved, and consummated only by sacrifice, then we have found the path of sanctity, for then we have entered into the luminous region of truth. Sorrow accompanies love in all its stages; and it does not do this as a companion that supports and guides, but as a part of its being, as the earthly aspect of that divine reality known as love.

In the life of love there are three great stages: the first prepares for union, the second consists in the union itself, and the third contains the prodigious consequences of this union which continues and grows more perfect. And to each of these three stages there corresponds a sorrow, or rather, a whole class of sorrows.

1. The Sorrow That Purifies

In the first stage, love snatches the soul from all things, even from itself, and places it in ineffable and magnificent solitude. Sacred Scripture says that love is as strong as death, which implacably snatches the soul from all things of this earth, and even separates it from the natural vesture with which it forms a single nature; for in this way love, powerful and implacable as death, continues to wrest the soul from everything earthly, and, after depriving it of external things, pierces like a two-edged sword into the depths of the soul, even unto the divisions of the soul and the spirit, according to the language of the Apostle, and consummates this mystical death which leaves the soul in immense and unspeakable solitude.

Even human love seizes and separates, and is akin to death; even human love requires solitude of heart for its consummation. The beloved is always chosen from among thousands, as is said in the Canticle. In order to encounter him, the heart had to withdraw from all things and to give up all things. Ordinarily we do not take account of the solitariness that love causes in our heart except when separation or death deprives us of that beloved object upon whom love centers our life and our being, after isolating us from all other things. Who has not felt this? The world has not changed, life follows its course, the sky remains blue, flowers diffuse their perfumes, birds sing, the sun warms and quickens, the same things surround us and the selfsame people associate with us. But alas, one thing is absent, one thing alone, and it is enough to make us feel lonely in the midst of a multitude, to induce a vast void into the soul, to make the earth appear to us a desert.

"A single being is away from us, yet it seems to us that the whole world has lost all its people." Thus spoke Lamartine. This is so because love has emptied the heart of everything and filled it with that whom we have chosen among thousands; and with the departure of the beloved, we feel alone with the deepest of lonelinesses in our heart.

Yet there is no comparison between the solitariness produced by human love and that which divine love demands; for there is no comparison between these two loves. Human love is shallow, divine love is profound; the first is partial and fragmentary, it never completely embraces the heart; the second is entire, absorbing, unparalleled. Human love has its own tint, and excludes at least all affections of that shade; but divine love embraces all colors, and consequently it excludes all loves. The jealousies of divine love are universal and implacable; that is why Sacred Scripture, after saying

that love is strong as death, adds: its jealousies are
terrible as hell.

Such deep and perfect solitude cannot be
achieved without sorrow, without a continual and
piercing sorrow. First of all, there are the sacrifices
of asceticism, which separate us from all things,
which pluck out of man everything that is per-
verse and merely human, which oppose all our inclinations, which dominate or moderate all our
tendencies. Then there is the great work of interior and exterior mortification, which perfect the
moral virtues in man: mortification, which dismays
and terrifies worldlings because they do not know
the secret of love. But we immolate ourselves; we
are at one and the same time priests and victims;
and upon the bloody altars of love we offer up all
things, and we sacrifice ourselves at the same time
as a fearful yet most sweet holocaust, a holocaust
to Him whom we have chosen among thousands,
to Him who wishes to be our One Alone, and whom
we freely and lovingly desire that He may be.

Afterwards, when our work has been completed,
we leave off being priests in order to conceal ourselves in the deep immolations of victims. Love
itself is the priest that offers us: keen and penetrat-
ing as a two-edged sword, it pierces to where we
would never be able to penetrate; it sinks its burning and painful darts into the deepest recesses of
the soul, into regions that we did not even suspect

existed in our being; and there it burns, and there it cuts, and there it plucks out and leaves on all sides the sharpest traces of an unknown sorrow; and it establishes everywhere the immense and ineffable solitude of love. There is no faculty that it does not touch, nor corner of the soul where it does not penetrate. Victorious and awe-inspiring, love passes into our whole being, from our external senses to our highest spiritual faculties, from our gross flesh that makes us akin with the brutes, to that mysterious center of our soul which makes us akin with God, since there it is that the immaterial and splendid image of the Trinity shines forth. Thus we understand how this entire first stage, which is filled with sorrow, purifies.

2. The Sorrow That Unites

When the soul is purified and free of all things earthly, it meets the Beloved in unfathomable solitude. Upon contemplating Him through the veil which always shields Him on this earth, but which becomes transparent in order that the soul may get a glimpse of the divine Beauty, the soul, all trembling with love and happiness, hurls itself toward Him with the eagerness of a desire that is soon to be fulfilled, with the impetuosity of its being that is touching upon its beatitude. Who can describe the ineffable embrace, the complete happiness of the soul that at length encounters Him whom it has loved? It is as a taste of heaven, as an irradiation of the eternal blessedness. How, then, can sorrow fit into that most sweet mystery?

No matter how close or perfect or intimate may be this union of God with the soul, it is not yet the consummated union of eternity; and everything that is lacking in this union on earth and that prevents it from attaining the perfection which the union in heaven possesses necessarily becomes sorrow that is mysteriously mixed with joy. This sorrow is something sweet and bitter at the same time, nevertheless a sorrow of an especial kind that surpasses in intensity all other sorrows. It is the more intense by how much the more it is pure, by how much the more it is spiritual, and by how much the more it is profound.

Love is insatiable; it is satisfied only with the infinite, satisfied only when it is possessed in that most perfect manner which is proper to heaven. Everything else serves but to excite desire and to convert it into a martyrdom. In the degree that anyone possesses God, he desires Him more; and the more intimate is the union, the more terrible is the martyrdom of desire. All mystics have spoken of this torturing desire that appeared more piercing to St. Theresa of Jesus than all the pains she had suffered, in spite of already having suffered very many.

But the desire for eternal union is not the only sorrow that accompanies union; there are other

sorrows, or if one prefers, other aspects of this sorrow that appears to confound itself with love itself.
Love's law is to establish a certain equality, a certain loving balance between those that love. By
its proper nature love demands that there be an
exchange of gifts, a mutual bestowing, a love for
love; and when such a balance is not achieved, the
eagerness to attain it turns into sorrow and martyrdom.

In the love of God, a disequilibrium is inevitable,
for how can the creature, poor and miserable, compete with an infinite love in intensity, a love that is
splendid in its gifts and divinely rich in tenderness?
Overwhelmed beneath the weight of infinite love,
the soul yearns, as St. Augustine did, to be God in
order to bestow Godlike gifts upon its Beloved; and
in the helplessness—cruel and sweet at the same
time, as everything is that pertains to love—to
compete with sovereign Love, the soul endeavors
to equalize the infinite riches of God with its own
infinitude, with the infinity of misery, and in its
audacity it wishes to supply with sorrow whatever
is lacking to its love to make it infinite.

Furthermore, there is, as it were, in the soul that
has arrived at union a secret and divine instinct
which gives it a presentiment that the supreme exchange of love cannot be realized on earth except
on condition the poor creature annihilate itself
and be consumed with sorrow. God gives Himself
in joy; and the angels give themselves without suf-

fering; perhaps in the earthly Paradise man knew the secret of giving himself in the midst of happiness unalloyed. But in the present state, in the supreme exchange of love, the most intense joy unites itself to the most profound sorrow, just as in the divine heart of Jesus the joy of the beatific vision is mysteriously mingled with the cruel sorrows that Sacred Scripture calls prophetically the sorrows of hell. And although the mystery of love can be realized on earth without having the soul converted into a victim and a holocaust in order to be conjoined with the Beloved, the fact that Jesus accomplished the supreme manifestation of love on the blessed cross should be sufficient for the souls that love Him to make them perceive the imperious necessity of suffering for Him, of giving themselves over to sorrow, of being overwhelmed with grief, and of being ground like wheat and pressed like grapes in the wine press in order to be converted into the food and drink of love, into a living Eucharist for the best Beloved.

Whether the world will believe it or not, whether the wise can explain it or not, the most gigantic and most eloquent deed that twenty centuries have witnessed consists in this: an uninterrupted host of souls delicately in love with their God seeking pain with a divine passion, with an avidity that joy has never been sought after; who have as their sole wish the cross, and who find in it a joy so hidden, a sweetness so heavenly, and a happiness so exquisite, that all proclaim with the ecstatic St. Francis of Assisi that perfect beatitude consists in suffering for the Blessed Christ.

3. The Sorrow That Redeems

We have now to consider the final degree of sorrow.

It is the nature of love to transform those who love, to the point of uniting them one to another in a certain manner. The words, "to have but one heart and one soul," are not mere hyperbole; they express a mystery of unity that all love achieves, since it effects that those who love one another have the same thoughts and the same affections, that their joys and their sorrows are shared in common. Sacred Scripture teaches us that this law of human love obtains in the divine, for St. Paul, with his customary boldness, instructs us as follows: "He who is joined to the Lord, is one spirit with Him." And Jesus, in the most solemn moments of His life, expresses His supreme desire and highest prayer to the heavenly Father in these words: "That they may be one, as We also are one. I in them, and Thou in Me; that they may be made perfect in one." [1]

The divine fruit of union is, therefore, transformation, the effecting of unity. Jesus lives in us, and we in Him. All that belongs to Him is ours, and

[1] John 17:22 f.

all that belongs to us is His: His joys are our joys, and His sorrows are our sorrows. Our acts become divine, and Jesus renews in us the mysteries of His life.

Among all the things that Jesus communicates to us and shares with us when we are transformed into Him, the foremost are His sorrows, His sacrifice; for His sorrows are most dear to Him, and sacrifice was the supreme act of His life. Avid of suffering, since His sufferings give glory to the Father and since they are the fountain of life for souls, Jesus did not remain content with the sufferings of His mortal life, but He wishes to continue them until the end of time in the Eucharist and in souls.

To the blessed souls that become one through love and that are transformed into Him, He shares His divine sufferings, His intimate sorrows, in order that He may continue suffering in them, as His insatiable desires demand, and in order that those souls might have divine sufferings whereby they may in due measure be glorifiers of the Father and redeemers of souls.

And here we touch upon the supreme secret of sorrow, a glimpse of which demands that we forsake the earth and plunge our spirit into the bosom of God. When it pleased the Father to give us His own Son, He gave to this Son of His eternal joys, to the Son whom He loves with an infinite and personal love in union with the Holy Ghost, He gave,

I say, as the highest proof of His love, as the most exquisite manifestation of His tenderness, the cross, with all the pains, ignominies, and bitterness involved in it. He sacrificed Him, He immolated Him, He "delivered Him up," says Sacred Scripture. What sorrow can this be that was the supreme gift of the infinite love of the Father for His incarnate Son? What can this sorrow be that is the highest gift of Jesus to the heavenly Father?

And since Jesus loves us in the same way that He is loved by the Father—"As the Father hath loved Me, I also have loved you" [2]—the supreme gift of the love of Jesus to souls is sorrow and the cross; for the supreme gift of the love of souls is this very cross that contains all the treasures of heaven and earth, since it embraces all the riches of love.

In the first degree, the sorrow that purifies is human, without ceasing to be supernatural; in the second degree, the unitive sorrow is heavenly by its purity and sublimity; but the sorrow of the third degree, glorifying and redeeming, is divine; it is the participation of the sorrow of Jesus and the reflection of the love of the Father.

The first seems to me to be symbolized by the ascent to Calvary; the second, by the exterior cross of Jesus upon which the souls that are crucified with Him unite themselves to Him in a most intimate embrace of love and of sorrow; and the last has for its emblem the innermost cross of the divine

[2] John 15:9.

heart of Jesus by which one rises to the Holy Spirit, the infinite and personal love of God, and the inexhaustible fount of all sorrowing love and of all loving sorrow.

VII

Love and Fruitfulness

▀▀

What a precious function is that of flowers: to diffuse their fragrance heavenward, and to place a fruitful seed upon the earth! What does it matter that their springtime is short and that their glory is transient; what does it matter that the richness of their petals vanishes as a passing dream, if their fragrance has sweetened the air, if their immortal seed is never to be lost?

Souls are like flowers. Beneath the richness of their virtues or beneath the fold of their miseries they conceal a divine perfume and a prolific seed. Their perfume is love; their virginal fecundity is Jesus, whom, in one way or other, they communicate to others. "The seed is the word of God." [1] I would be so bold as to translate: "The seed is the Word of God." In all true and immortal fecundity, the seed is the Word of God: in its reflection, in its image, in its divine and mysterious reproduction. In taking upon Himself human flesh, the Word of God became a divine Gardener. Enamored of

[1] Luke 8:11.

souls, He sows the seed from heaven without tiring, breathes in the exquisite fragrance of their flowers when they come to bloom, and lovingly gathers up the rich nectar.

What is there in souls that makes Jesus love them so? What is that divine fragrance that they harbor in their mysterious bosom? Who can understand that divine something that the Creator infused in them with His omnipotent breath, that Jesus watered with His precious blood, that the Holy Ghost nourishes with His sanctifying overshadowing?

Perhaps the springtime of souls may also be transient, and hasten away with its unforgettable enchantments, its heavenly musing, its immaculate freshness. But what does it matter if souls, like flowers, upon coming to their autumnal bloom, realize their precious destiny: to diffuse their divine fragrance heavenward, and to place their immortal seed upon other souls? For the perfume is for heaven, and the seed is for earth. In reality, all is for Jesus, the divine Gardener. For whom are souls if not for Him? Jesus breathes in the perfume and retains it in His heart, and He lays up the nectar in His storehouses in order to nourish souls.

Love, which is the perfume of souls, is for the intimate service of Jesus; it is a loving gift for Him; it is to enrich the alabaster vase of His heart which is ever dilated and ever eager for the perfume that is perpetually diffused and never exhausted. The fruitfulness, however, is for souls, that they may bud forth new flowers, that they may continue diffusing perfumes over the earth, and that the divine Gardener may continue to be enraptured with the exquisite fragrance of love. Every soul ought to emit its heavenly fragrances in the garden of the Beloved, and every soul ought to deposit on other souls the seeds of its virginal fruitfulness.

Flowers exhale their most exquisite and precious perfume only when their petals undergo change upon withering, or when they are crushed to draw out the treasure of their most exquisite essence. One could say that in the glory of their springtime they diffuse only a superficial fragrance, but that they avariciously retain in their uttermost depth their hidden fragrance, which they do not emit until wounded by death, whereupon they allow the precious vessels that enclose their treasure to be opened or taken from them. It is said that the myrrh tree allows its perfume to escape only when it is bruised. The same thing occurs with other aromatic gums, which flow drop by drop through the lacerations of the bark that enfolds them.

So it is with souls. They can readily diffuse their ordinary fragrance in shallow affections. How many emit it prodigally, without grief and without effort, in the heyday of their springtide joy! Happy are they who never waste their divine riches, but who with loving care save all the treasures of their tenderness for their divine Gardener!

But souls possess another perfume, which is far below the surface, exquisite, concentrated. It is a love confected in the mysterious center of the soul —how many there are who do not even suspect their wealth!—a love that upon being liberated penetrates and transforms the entire soul, converting it into pure love, and making it unsuitable for everything that is not true love. It is passion; it is folly; it is beatitude; it is I know not what divine thing that human words can never explain. It is a most sweet secret that many blessed souls can feel, but which none can express, because it is inexpressible.

This heavenly perfume is what the divine Jesus, who profoundly knows His flowers, is desirous to breathe in. He goes so far as to allow the enemy to sow tares in His garden, and to permit that the hurricane come at some time or other to lay waste His enclosure. And even though He weeps over the faded flowers and the broken stems, He remains satisfied if only some few flowers have emerged victorious over the tares and the storm in order to confect for Him the exquisite and desired perfume.

But no soul emits this mysterious fragrance if it is not wounded by sorrow; if it does not allow its rich petals to fade and to be pressed; if it does not allow the secret folds that conceal the divine to be cruelly rent. For this reason many souls, yes, very many, pass their life without knowing how to love, believing that their selfish and empty affections are love; thinking that all their fragrance is diffused in the easy expansion of their shallow affections. They do not know how to love, because they do not know how to suffer, because they are even unaware of the secret of profound love, because, either unknowing or faint-hearted, they wish to love with an ephemeral happiness and a transient joy. And they do not even suspect that true happiness conceals itself in sorrow, that perfect joy cannot blossom except in profound love, whose celestial drops are distilled only through the deep, wide gashes of sorrow.

Hence there are so few happy souls; for few are they that love, and few are they that give themselves without reserve to sorrow in order that the alabaster vase which contains the perfume may be broken and that thus love may diffuse itself and inebriate the entire soul with the heavenly and blessed sweetness of true charity.

Jesus taught us that happiness consists solely in sorrow, since it is rooted solely in love. The saints have repeated this to us as the fruit of their blessed experience. Not even yet have the celestial accents of a soul of our own time that has inebriated the Church with the sweetness of her perfumes faded away. Even now we seem to hear as harmony from heaven the angelic voice of the virgin of Lisieux, which sings: "I shall find happiness and joy on earth, but only in suffering." [2]

But the world does not hear this doctrine, nor does it wish to listen to it. Hence many souls keep seeking after love and happiness where they do not find them, where they cannot find them; and they prodigally and foolishly allow the perfume of their shallow affections to dissipate itself. Eager for happiness, they seek it in pleasures that have been multiplied and refined by a false modern culture, without understanding that everything which increases pleasure increases self-love, and that self-love is the eternal enemy of love and of happiness, since it is the enemy of sorrow. They pursue their quest without realizing that the sad and painful attempts they make to be happy serve only to put them farther away from happiness, since they choke off in their profoundest depth, whose existence they do not even dimly realize, the source of true love, the only love that contains the secret of happiness.

Thanks be to God for the hidden souls that have received or are disposed to receive the divine revelation about sorrow. These the divine Jesus cultivates with tenderness in His gardens; upon them He turns the stream of His graces and the springtime glory of His counsels; He prepares them for the fruitful maturity of autumn, and, when the mo-

[2] *Novissima Verba,* p. 102.

ment arrives, He will send His loving messenger, sorrow, to wound His flowers of predilection. Then He Himself with His divine hands—for to no one else will He confide the loving and delicate work—will lovingly pierce the innermost folds that contain the treasure and bring forth the exquisite perfume. And Jesus will inhale it and preserve it in His heart; and the soul will rejoice for having emitted it, and will be changed into the most pure love, and will rejoice upon the cross of Christ with the only happiness that one can rejoice with upon the earth.

Jesus wounds souls because He loves them, because He wishes that they give Him their fragrance, because He desires to make them happy. If there were anything better than sorrow, He would bestow it upon them; but, in accordance with His loving designs, there does not exist on earth any better incentive of love and any more precious means of happiness than sorrow. To give us all His love, He Himself embraced the cross. What is the mystery of Calvary but the divine vessel of the heart of Jesus crushed by sorrow in order to fill the earth with the perfume of His immense love?

What Magdalen did in anointing the feet of Jesus with the exquisite essence of spikenard will ever be the eternal symbol of perfect love.

I do not know whether the perfume of flowers has any relation to their fruitfulness, but I do know that in the case of souls fruitfulness is the logical consequence of love. In the spiritual order the only fecund thing is love. Words are empty and works sterile when they are not the fruit of love, when they are not impregnated with the divine fragrance. The measure of a soul's fruitfulness is its love. For this reason St. Paul teaches that without love the speaking with the tongues of angels and of men is as vain and as unenduring as the sounding of a bell, and that the greatest works, even martyrdom, are sterile.

But that love should produce its fruit, it needs sorrow. The divine Master told us expressly of this indispensable condition of fruitfulness: "Unless the grain of wheat falling into the ground die, itself remaineth alone. But if it die, it bringeth forth much fruit." [3] Pleasure stands condemned to a sad isolation; self-love is sterile. Only sorrow possesses the divine privilege of multiplying itself; its fruitfulness is the expansion of love into martyrdom.

To do good to souls we must suffer for them; we must love them as Jesus did, and like Him be nailed to the cross for them.

"Prayer and sacrifice constitute my strength; they are my invincible arms. They, more than words, can touch hearts: this I know from experience," wrote St. Theresa of the Child Jesus in explaining the good that she did for her novices. [4] Let

[3] John 12:24 f.
[4] *Histoire d' une âme*, chap. 10.

us not build up illusions; there is no other force, there are no other arms, wherewith to do good, wherewith to give to Jesus.

Whoever feels the divine fire of zeal for souls in his heart, whoever desires the supreme joys of spiritual fruitfulness, let him be converted into that little bundle formed by the fragrances of incense and of myrrh of which the Canticle speaks; let him wisely merge, in the interior of his soul, the aroma of love with the fragrance of sacrifice.

O Jesus, divine Gardener! We are flowers born in the garden of Thy Church and watered with Thy precious blood. Spikenard or lilies, roses or violets, exquisite flowers or simple blooms of the field, we have received from Thee the richness of our petals, the treasures of our perfumes, and the blessing of our fruitfulness. We wish to live for Thee in the corner of Thy garden, where Thy divine hand has planted us; and we yearn to realize our precious destiny: to send our fragrance of love heavenward in order that Thou mayest inhale it and repose it in Thy heart; and to place the fruitful seed upon souls.

Send us Thy Spirit that His vivifying overshadowing may enlarge our heart. Nail us to Thy cross, and when we have been fixed there, wound us with Thy loving hand in order that the concentrated and exquisite fragrance of perfect love may issue forth from the depth of our heart; in order that the divine seeds of our fruitfulness may fall upon souls, as the fragrance of eternal love was diffused from Thy crushed heart, and as the precious drops of Thy blood flowed from Thy sweet wounds.

VIII

Fragrance and Bitterness

▬▬▬

"A bundle of myrrh is my beloved to me" (Cant. 1:12).

"A bundle of myrrh is my beloved to me," exclaims the Spouse of the Canticles. Bitter and fragrant is myrrh. Bitterness and fragrance is Jesus to my soul. Love—yes; it is a fragrance. And is it not a most sweet and precious fragrance? O fragrance that diffuses itself, O fragrance that enters even into the heart and causes a divine intoxication! Christ came to the world to diffuse this divine fragrance of love and to inebriate the earth with it. He is a fragrance for God. God takes pleasure in inhaling the good odor of Christ. Christ is a fragrance for men. When He appeared, men saw themselves wrapped in a celestial atmosphere of love. He is principally a fragrance for the souls of predilection, for those upon whom God in His most loving designs has freely poured forth the perfume of His love.

But the fragrance of Christ is like the myrrh. "Myrrh," says Fray Luis de Leon, "is a tiny tree that grows in Arabia, Egypt, and Judea, which, when its bark is pierced at certain seasons, distills that substance which we call myrrh." It is by wounding this tree that its fragrance is emitted.

The love of Christ flows chiefly from His wounds, from His suffering. At the commencement of His life Christ was wounded; hence He diffused His fragrance from the beginning. But in the Passion He was wounded completely; He was but a single wound. Hence on the cross His love, as a strong and exquisite perfume that escapes from the vessel of alabaster that holds it, was diffused over heaven and earth. God was infinitely well pleased with the love of His Christ, and we were convinced of the love of God.

The eruption of the loving perfume—let us call it that—Christ wished to perpetuate through all ages in the Eucharist. And this sacrament is a bundle of myrrh; here also emanates the fragrance of the wounds. If the Eucharist is a marvel of love, that is because it is a marvelous sacrifice. Everywhere, on Calvary and in the Eucharist, the fragrance of love is diffused through open wounds, through sacrifice.

The Church, which is Christ perpetuating Himself on earth, is a bundle of myrrh. When persecutions wound her—and persecutions are never wanting, thanks be to God—she profusely radiates the good odor of Christ in all directions. A period of persecution is a period of love, a period of saints.

Sanctity, which is love, is the fragrance that springs from the mystical body of Christ when enemies wound it. Love, we know, unites, assimilates, and unifies those who love one another: souls that love Christ are like unto Him, a bundle of myrrh; with them as with Christ, fragrance emanates from wounds.

Let us continue the comparison. Let us imagine a fragrance so strong that it could of itself make an opening in the vessel that contains it, and then upon emerging through the opening could enlarge it so that this opening, becoming greater, would allow more fragrance to escape. What would happen? The fragrance would keep breaking up the vessel; and the vessel would keep allowing more fragrance to escape in the measure that it became more broken up, until the vessel would be wasted away and the fragrance would have diffused itself in its entirety. Love causes a wound, and the wound produces an increase of love; then love opens the wound wider, and the wound in turn increases the love, until the soul becomes a single wound, that is, pure love. The vessel will ultimately disappear, and love alone will remain. Thus will the soul become deified.

Now I ask you: What is sweeter, the love or the wound? What is more desirable, the fragrance or the bitterness of the myrrh?

IX

The Secrets of the Interior Life

▪▪

1

There is nothing so important in the supernatural order as to have a deep, intense interior life. This is so, because at times we run into the error of subordinating the interior life to the practice of the virtues, as if our contact with God were only a means to perfect ourselves.[1]

[1] This error is more common than appears at first sight. One author, highly recommendable, it is true, in a work of his written for priests, has, nevertheless, expressions like these: "Everything in prayer ought to converge to the resolution and contribute in a definite way toward the reform or the perfecting of one's life." "The resolution is the immediate term of prayer; its final end is the effective reform or perfecting of one's life through the fulfillment of the resolution." "Prayer is the laboratory of the soul's resolution." "In prayer there is no question of art for art's sake, but of working to make resolves and thus eventually to better one's life." Cannot this be called spiritual utilitarianism?

Reform of life is a means of bettering prayer, and at the same time it is its fruitful and happy result; but the immediate end of prayer is our union with God, and its final end is the glory of God. An artist, a painter, for example, needs money to exercise his art, at least to obtain the materials (paints, brushes, canvas, and the like), and with his art he is able to earn money, perhaps even a great deal of

The case is not thus. There is no doubt that prayer and all the other acts of the interior life have an efficacious influence on the acquistion of the virtues. From our relation with God we draw the strength wherewith to repel temptations, self-knowledge whereby to be humble, sweetness of temper wherewith to treat with our neighbors, and the light and the strength with which to practice all the other virtues. Even more can be said, for one may be sure that the virtues which do not have their roots in the interior life are neither solid nor deep.

But this does not mean to say that we approach God solely to acquire virtues. On the contrary, the active life and all the virtues that we must practice with respect to our neighbor and to ourselves, more than being the reward of our efforts, are the means whereby to achieve the contemplative life, the perfect interior life. In other words, the contemplative life is not a means or a ladder whereby to arrive at the active life. On the contrary, we work, we struggle, we sacrifice ourselves in order to love God, in order to have intimate and loving relations with Him. The true spiritual life consists in our relations with God. Relations with the neighbor and even with ourselves are something secondary; either they are ordinated to achieve the interior life, or they are an overflowing from it.

money. But who is going to say that because of this the end of art is commercial? We must think in the same way when we treat of prayer, of the interior life.

But the central point of the spiritual life is the contemplative life. Why? Because it is for this that God made us. He made us for Himself, that we might know Him, love Him, and serve Him. Hence if we sacrifice ourselves to achieve a betterment of our life and conduct, it is solely that we may render ourselves worthy to have intercourse with God. Thus our interior life is the summit, the ideal, the goal toward which all our efforts ought to converge.

The contemplative life is the life of heaven. There all the works of the active life will disappear. In heaven there will be no passions to contend with, nor neighbors to help, nor miseries to bear. The life of the blessed is an eternal contemplation: they see God, love Him and are united to Him in an indissoluble embrace. This is the true life.

And God in His goodness has desired that even in this life we should exercise ourselves in that which will constitute our eternal life. Already here below we can contemplate Him, although in the mists of faith; already here below we can love Him, and with the same love of heaven, although it does not produce in us the same effects as in the blessed. This is the true life; all else is fading and transitory. For this reason our Lord told Martha that she was concerned about many things when only one thing was necessary and, on the other hand, that Mary had chosen the better part, and that it would never be taken from her. In this way our Lord Himself teaches us that the contemplative life is better than the active, and that it will never be taken from the soul that has chosen it.

It is the better part because it is the most exalted. To live with God, to know Him, and to love Him is the highest activity that a creature can exercise; not even the seraphim can aspire to anything more exalted. It is the better part because it is the most excellent. What is more excellent than to have intercourse with God and to be friends and intimates with the Supreme Being? And no one can take it away from us. The active life is solely of time; the contemplative life is eternal. The life of mortification of the great penitents, the apostolic life of the great apostles, the priestly ministry, no matter how holy and fruitful it may be, end with death; only one thing does not cease: the contemplative life. It continues on in heaven; it is eternal.

The life of an artist, for example, consists in contemplating and reproducing beauty according to his proper art. He can do other things, as when he takes a vacation. But this is only a passing diversion. For when the journey has ended and the unwonted circumstances have changed, he will return to his art, which for him is his chief concern. All else is secondary and of passing moment.

Thus it is with us. We have been elevated to the supernatural order to contemplate God and to love Him. God created us for heaven. To be sure, while we travel on the earth we have to do many other things: combat our passions, help our neighbor, and so on. But these are not the proper activity of our life; they are secondary things that pass away. Our Lord wishes that our chief occupation on earth should be to exercise ourselves in what is to be our everlasting occupation in heaven: to contemplate Him and love Him. We shall not be able to do this with the fullness and perfection with which the blessed do it; but, at the least, in the midst of the preoccupations of this life, we ought to give the better part to the interior life. This, then, is the only true life. Hence whatever else we do avails only to the extent that it is penetrated with the interior life, with the savor of contemplation.

We who have an exterior ministry, such as priests and members of Catholic Action, cannot do good for souls if we do not possess an intense interior life, as Dom Chautard has amply demonstrated in his work, *The Soul of the Apostolate.* "We are the good odor of Christ," says St. Paul, and for its diffusion in all directions, it is indispensable that we be deeply penetrated with Him and united to Him, that is, that we have an intense interior life. Souls that cannot exercise any activity directly upon their neighbors ought, from the recesses of their retirement, to diffuse the graces of God upon others. But they will be able to do this only to the extent that they possess an intense interior life.

The true efficacy of our works depends upon our interior life, and the true worth of a soul is the worth of its interior life; for a soul's worth is in direct proportion to the intimacy and intensity of its relations with God. The interior life is the chief, the most important, and the most efficacious element of the spiritual life. It is the one thing necessary.

Hence this is the great problem for every soul that aspires after perfection: What shall I do that my interior life may be deeper and more intense? It is very likely that each of my readers possesses the interior life in his soul. But no one can be satisfied with the spiritual life that he has; in our present state we always have need for more, and we can never say, "Now I have enough."

What I say of the spiritual order applies to all orders; it is a very human trait never to be satiated with that which we love. When is the artist ever satiated with beauty? When does the savant feel satiated with truth? This is true because in our heart we have something that is infinite: our desires. Material things weary us. The glutton can eat a great deal, but the moment arrives when it becomes repugnant to him to continue eating: he becomes full, he can eat no more. With spiritual things it is not thus, even in the natural order. On earth, he that loves, desires to love more; the learned man does not tire of investigating truth, nor does the artist in contemplating and reproducing it. Every noble and exalted human life is above satiation. With greater reason is this true of the spiritual life. Consequently, no matter how intense the interior life of a soul may be, it needs more and aspires to more.

And since the interior life is nothing else but our relations with God, our intimate and loving intercourse with Him, the problem becomes this: What shall we do that our intercourse with Him may become more intimate and our relations with Him more intense? This is the purpose of these chapters: to solve this problem; to investigate with the light of the Holy Ghost what is necessary that our interior life may be more intense and more profound.

2

The problem that we have to solve, then, is this: How shall we proceed that our interior life may become more intense day by day, and thus be able to realize our ideal and fulfill our purpose in life? Now to solve the problem I propose, not so much to give rules, or to make observations, or to suggest isolated helps, as to disclose the key that will basically resolve the problem. To this end it will be a good idea, first of all, to state it clearly and precisely.

There are periods in which the interior life becomes easy and sweet. Who has not had times, more or less extended, when he was able, without any difficulty, to live for days filled with fervor? The pity is that we have not been able to determine why or how we arrived at this state. One fine day we perceived ourselves recollected; the presence of God became very easy for us; our soul was at rest, and we enjoyed a period of peace. But the next day everything faded away, and we did not know how the fervor came or how it departed. And, unfortunately, since the bright days are few and the overcast ones are more frequent, we do not know, by a fixed rule, over many and long periods of time, what we must do to cultivate the interior life. Some souls even believe that fervor is a sort of lottery prize: he whose turn it is to win, wins, and he whose turn it is not, has nothing to do but to resign himself. If we could only discover the thread of this labyrinth, the key of the interior life, so that we might know what we have to do both in the bright days and in the clouded and overcast ones! We might attempt to solve the problem in a superficial manner and enumerate all the elements whence the interior life takes its origin. For example: interior and exterior recollection; overcoming of self-love; purity of the heart which ought to be empty of all created things; the practice of the virtues; and so on. Thus the problem would be solved by saying that the soul must have and must intensify all these elements in order that the interior life might grow and develop.

But the question would still stand, and the soul would ask anew: How does one acquire recollection, empty the heart, and practice the virtues? For, many times the soul desires recollection and cannot achieve it. Neither can anyone empty the heart perfectly except by filling it with God through the medium of the interior life; nor can anyone practice the virtues perfectly except by holding before the eyes of the soul the divine Model, whom we contemplate in prayer. Hence we do not so much need to know the elements of the interior life and the means that favor it as to discover the key, the central point, that solves the whole difficulty. Where is this key of the interior life? May God be pleased to reveal the secret to us!

First of all we must have clear ideas about the interior life. The spiritual life consists essentially in charity; and Christian perfection is nothing else but the plenitude of charity. Now, charity has two aspects: love of God and love of the neighbor. Hence the interior life consists in love of God and love of the neighbor: principally in love of God and secondarily in love of the neighbor. Therefore to live the spiritual life is to love God above all things and the neighbor as ourselves. When we come to love in this way, we completely fulfill the law. "Love therefore is the fulfilling of the law." [2]

From this double aspect of charity, the love of God and the love of the neighbor, flow the two forms of the spiritual life: the contemplative life and the active life. The contemplative life embraces all our relations with God, which consist essentially in knowing and loving Him. The active life embraces everything that has a relationship with our neighbor, such things, for example, as the practice of the moral virtues and the works of mercy.

The legitimate love of ourselves is contained in the love of our neighbor: the first of our neighbors is ourselves. Furthermore, the model and type of love that we should have for others is the legitimate love that we have for ourselves. "Thou shalt love thy neighbor as thyself."

The love of the neighbor, moreover, has a twofold aspect. One is to make use of the neighbor to go to God, using him as a means to unite ourselves with God. The other is to serve the neighbor. Thus, once we are united to God we can descend to the neighbor to bring him the graces that we have obtained in our contact with the Supreme Being. Intercourse with the neighbor is a profitable occasion wherein to exercise many virtues that bring us to God, such as humility, mortification, self-abnegation, patience, meek-

[2] Rom. 13:10.

ness. For this reason St. Thomas says that, for achieving perfection, life with our brethren is better than the eremitical life; but as soon as one has achieved perfection, the eremitical life is better than the life in company with others.

And we have already indicated the reason for this; for it is our contact with the neighbor that gives us the opportunity to practice many virtues. If we lived in the desert, we would perhaps not suspect many of our weaknesses. The neighbor humbles us and thus exposes our pride and self-love; with his impertinences he reveals our irascibility or makes us practice meekness; with his manifold demands he forces us to practice self-abnegation or brings to light our self-love; and so on. For this reason spiritual writers say that the active life is the preparation for the contemplative life, because in the former we exercise the virtues that dispose us for the latter.

But once we have ascended to the summit of the contemplative life, traveling up the side which is the active life, we come down on the other side, bearing in our hands the treasures of God to distribute to the neighbor. This is the apostolic life. There is no one that has arrived at union with God, at the plenitude of contemplation, that does not feel himself eaten up with zeal for the salvation of souls. Then he descends from the height of contemplation to the field of the apostolate to win souls for God.

Summary: The contemplative life has God as its object; the active life concerns itself with the neighbor. When this life is the overflowing of the contemplative life, it is called the apostolic life. And this is the most perfect, since it supposes the plenitude of contemplation and the perfection of activity: it is, as it were, a synthesis of the active life and the contemplative life.

With respect to the neighbor, we have no need to contemplate him, but only to serve him or to avail ourselves of him to go to God. With respect to God, on the contrary, we have only to contemplate and to love Him; for contemplation and love merge into one single divine effect: union and deification. Hence the interior life at its apex is the contemplative life. And far from being something monotonous and wearisome, it is most varied and inexhaustible: eternity itself will not be long enough to exhaust the treasures of light and of beauty that are found in God; much less shall we be able to exhaust them in this world.

There are some saints who appear to know only one thing, who on all sides see only one thing. Some regard only the nothingness of creatures and the "all" of God; others reflect only on this or that passage of the Gospel; still others fix their gaze on a mystery of the life of Christ or on an attribute of divinity. And it does not cause us wonderment that they do not concern themselves with anything else. Each of the mysteries of God, each of His attributes, each facet of His divine countenance, is sufficient to consume an entire life.

In one manner or another, therefore, every interior life must in its final phase be the contemplative life. Well, then, to contemplate God the first requisite is to encounter Him. And once we have encountered Him, we need to know the means whereby to enter into communication with Him.

If I have a great desire to hear the lectures of a master, but if I do not know in what country or in what city he lives, the first thing I need to do is to search for him. And once I have found him, it is indispensable to know the language he speaks so that I may enter into communication with him. The same thing occurs in the interior life. All its secrets consist in this: to know how to find God and to know how to enter into communication with Him. All this seems to be the most simple and obvious thing in the world. For where is God? We do not have to ascend to heaven to find Him. God is within us: "In Him we live, and move, and are." [3] The divine Goodness has wished to remain with us, in our heart and in the tabernacle. Yet despite bearing God in our heart, and living in a divine atmosphere, and having

[3] Acts 17:28.

Him in the tabernacle, how difficult it ever is to find God! Is not this not-finding God the great torment of souls?

It seems that it should be an easy and simple thing to enter into communion with Him. Does He not speak all tongues? Does He not penetrate to the very depth of our hearts? We do not even have to open our lips; it suffices that we open our heart, it suffices that we love. Furthermore, we know that He is ever seeking us, that He is eager to enter into communion with us. What mystery is this?

If all people—the wise, the ignorant, the simple, the imperfect, and even the sinners—have the right to enter into communication with God, why is it difficult to do so in practice? The answer lies in this frequent complaint of pious souls: "I cannot pray."

"How so, if prayer is, as it were, the breath of the soul?"

"That is true; I feel the need to pray; I wish to do so; but I am not able. I cannot form a single act. I am dumb, deaf, dry; I cannot hear, nor speak, nor feel."

How can one explain these apparent contradictions? God stands near, yet we do not find Him. We can enter into communication with Him in all manner of ways, yet we do not succeed in doing so.

Here we meet with the key of the interior life.

The explanation of these apparent contradictions lies in this, that our God is a hidden God, as the Sacred Scriptures tell us. "Verily Thou art a hidden God." [4] And a hidden God must be sought. If there is a secret hiding place in a room, and if there is a person concealed in it, we do not encounter him, even though he is near us. We do not even suspect his presence. Thus it is with God. He is a hidden God. He is present everywhere, but everywhere He is concealed: in the stars of the heavens, in the earth that supports us, in the air that we breathe, in the neighbors that surround us. But will we always discover God?

As pertains to the saints, yes. They find God everywhere; and for that reason some of them went into ecstasy before a simple flower, since they discovered God in it. We, on the other hand, need to make innumerable reasonings to know that He is there. As our faith tells us, God lives in our heart. But sad experience teaches us that we do not always encounter Him. Why? Because, although He is there, He is hidden; and to find a hidden person, it is necessary to seek him. God is in the Eucharist in a special way; and of all the places where He is, there we encounter Him most easily. However, even there He is hidden. How often we draw near to the tabernacle without perceiving or feeling anything!

Consequently one of the secrets of the interior

[4] Isa. 45:15.

life consists, not in knowing where God is, because we already know that He is everywhere, but in knowing that, wherever He is, He is hidden. Hence the secret of entering into communication with Him is to find Him.

The second secret is this: once we have found God, how do we communicate with Him? Sacred Scripture tells us: "For My thoughts are not your thoughts: nor your ways My ways, saith the Lord." [5] Herein is the source of our difficulty in communicating with Him; for His thoughts are not our thoughts, nor are His ways our ways. Thus God communicates to us through one way, and we walk in another. He has His manner of approaching us, and we do not understand, for in reality we wish that He would communicate with us in our way. For example, we believe that as often as God communicates with us, we must feel it, since we cannot imagine that communication with a beloved person, as our Lord is, could be dry and barren. But since the ways of God are different from ours, ninety-nine percent of the times that our Lord comes to us, we do not feel it. And this deludes us, and we believe we cannot communicate with our Lord because we cannot perceive Him.

To us it seems that our Lord can have only a delicious sweetness, and that when He comes we must, therefore, taste Him with the sweetness of

[5] Is. 55:8.

the blessed. And sometimes it is thus. The coming of our Lord fills our hearts with sweetness. But God does not always taste the same. He is like the manna; He holds within Himself all savors.

St. Bernardine of Siena says that God has two savors: the savor of sweetness and the savor of bitterness. When we feel our heart heavy, it is also God who draws near; it is Jesus who communicates with us—no matter how poorly we understand that He also possesses the savor of bitterness. Well does St. Thomas say that all our errors in the spiritual life flow from this, that we wish to measure divine things with our human criterion, which is so puny and paltry. How often, when we think that we are most distant from God, we are most closely united to Him!

According to my view, the secret and key of the interior life is this: Jesus is a hidden God; we must therefore seek Him. But in seeking Him we must remember that the ways of God are very different from our ways. To know those ways and to seek God through them are the sole means of finding God and of uniting ourselves to Him.

3

The first reason why it is difficult for us to communicate with God is this: He is "a hidden God." He has always been thus, even in the days of His mortal life. How often we grieve over not having lived in the time when Jesus was on this earth! Then we would have known and loved Him, and we would have lived with Him. But even then it was not so easy to know Jesus. How many saw Him, heard His words of eternal life, and looked upon Him with mortal eyes, and yet how few really understood Him and loved Him! Even His very apostles, who had such intimate contact with Him, how imperfectly they understood Him and loved Him before the Passion! And why? Because always, even in the days of His mortal life, Jesus is a hidden God. But He conceals Himself that we may seek Him, and to those who seek Him, He manifests Himself clearly, as the Scripture tells us.

How does one seek Jesus? How does one find Him? First of all, there are eyes that always find Him, because they discover Him wherever He is, and no matter how hidden He may be; they are the eyes of faith. Faith penetrates all recesses and finds God behind all concealments; our Lord can hide Himself from all things except faith. It is like the X-rays that pierce opaque bodies and bring their interior to light; or like those instruments which, as we are told, indicate where treasures are located.

Faith never fails, it never errs, it is infallible. But since it is obscure, it rarely satisfies. And we should like to find Jesus, but in our own way, for our thoughts are not His thoughts, nor our ways His ways. For this reason St. John of the Cross says that the great means of arriving at contemplation is obscure faith. The core of the saint's teaching is that we must go to God by obscure faith without any sensible pleasure. But it is a way that is not pleasing to us, since we should like to feel God's presence and enjoy His sensible consolations.

There is no doubt that at times our Lord conjoins consolations with faith, which then make its exercise most easy for us; but it is not good that this should always occur. It is not good for us because we would never arrive at perfection by the way of consolations; it is not good for our Lord, because then He would not be able to accomplish His loving designs. Therefore He is so sparing in consolations; it is not because He does not love us—for of Himself He would always have us in a heaven—but precisely because He does love us. And when God dispenses and measures His consolations to souls, He should be more sparing with those who have the mission to console Him. For as an athlete does not strengthen and train himself in a pleasant idleness, but in hard and strenuous exercises, so a soul that would console our Lord cannot prepare itself to fulfill its mission by receiving consolations, but by seeing itself deprived of them.

After all, if we would consider things well, we would not have an avidity for consolations. For do we really know what is needful for our sanctification? We are so dull that, as St. Paul says, we do not know what we should ask for; we do not even know what we ought to desire. It would be stupidity to wish to govern our own destiny and to say: Now I need consolation; now aridity. Let us leave to God, who loves us, the work of forming us.

A story is told of a husbandman who besought God to allow that the rains, the sun, and all the elements be subject to his desires, and that there never be any storm. God granted this to him, and the husbandman said: Now I need rain, and it rained; now sun, and the sun came out resplendently. And, in the end, after a whole year in spite of those extraordinary powers that had been granted him, the harvest was lost.

"Lord," the husbandman then said; "what happened?"

"You besought everything," our Lord answered him, "and everything was granted you. But you did not ask for storms, and storms are necessary that the seed may germinate and develop."

The same thing would occur with us. We would ask for everything except storms: drynesses and desolations. And if we should ask for them it would be rarely, not understanding that they are necessary in order that the divine seed may germinate and develop in the soil of our heart. The best thing is to place ourselves in the hands of God, that He may give us His grace and His love; and that, as St. Ignatius says, ought to be sufficient for us.

There is no doubt that consolations are good, provided that God gives them; but they are dangerous. Since we cling to them very easily, from the very start our heart needs to be detached from everything, even from spiritual comforts, if we would unite ourselves to God. The only thing that the heart should attach itself to is God. Created things always contain a dangerous element, for in attaching ourselves to them we withdraw from God. And even the graces of God are created things.

In our lifetime we have heard mention made of the different classes of virtues: common, spiritual, and spiritually perfect. The common or ordinary virtues detach us from the ordinary things of life, such as all external and material things, the goods of fortune, fame, honor, esteem, friendship. Spiritual virtues detach us from those little things which, as it were, hold an intermediate place, such as between the soul and the body, or between heaven and earth: for example, sensible consolations in prayer and in spiritual exercises. The spiritually perfect virtues detach us from even the smallest, most subtle, and most spiritual things. They are the virtues that oppose the spiritual vices which St. John of the Cross speaks of, such as

spiritual pride, spiritual gluttony, spiritual **ava-**
rice, defects that are common to souls advanced
in the path of perfection.

Another danger of consolations, one that is
closely connected with the foregoing, is this:
When we have become habituated to seeking God
in the midst of consolations, we forget the most
high wisdom of seeking God in the midst of sorrow. If illumination by electricity were completely
to disappear, and if we would have to return to
illumination by candles, we would find it hard to
grow accustomed to this faulty lighting, and we
would always be missing the other. The same
thing occurs to us when we grow accustomed to
seek God in consolations; henceforth we do not
wish to seek Him by any other way.

Hence our Lord multiplies desolations and cur-
tails sensible delights in order that we accustom
ourselves to seek Him in the obscurity of the faith,
of the faith that never fails us and that always
leads to Jesus. Consequently one of the secrets of
the interior life is to seek Jesus by means of faith.

4

It is not my intention at this time to speak of
the importance that the spirit of faith has in the
spiritual life, or of the necessity of judging everything with a supernatural rule, or of performing
all our works with aims and intentions of the same

order. This is what I wish to insist upon and to
call attention to in an emphatic manner: the chief
reason why we disregard faith is our preconceived
idea that we must feel God and divine things.
Although we know speculatively that God is not
felt, practically we hold the contrary. We believe
that the true story of our spiritual life is made up
of all those things that we have sensibly experienced. Nothing is more erroneous. The spiritual
life is not perceived by the senses. Do we feel the
increase of grace in our soul? Do we feel a sacrament producing its proper effect? Do we feel the
death of the soul by sin and its resurrection by
sacramental absolution? Do we feel the real presence of Jesus in the Eucharist in such a way that
if we did not perceive Him sensibly we would not
believe in it?

Without doubt there are times when our Lord
allows Himself to be sensibly felt; yet it is not
precisely grace that is felt, but often something
else that accompanies it. For example: we go to
confession to a priest who simply listens to the
sins, gives a penance, and absolves; and we feel
nothing. We go to another who understands us,
who helps us in our disclosures to him, who gives
us helpful advice; and we feel such a peace and
refreshment that upon arising we seem to be other
beings. Was it the grace of the sacrament that we
felt? No; it was the profitable experience that we
had with the second priest.

Undoubtedly there are also stages in the spiritual life in which one becomes aware of it, at least momentarily. But to be conscious of a thing and to feel it sensibly is not the same thing; neither is one's whole spiritual life a thing of continual conscious awareness. If we read the life of St. Theresa of the Child Jesus with attention, we shall be convinced that she experienced delight only a very few times in her spiritual life, and that she rarely enjoyed the sensible consolations which we are considering. She lived by faith, by the obscurity of faith, and she is one of the most marvelous examples of that life of faith. In the midst of desolations, doubts, and terrible struggles, she always maintained an intense interior life. She is one of the few souls that aridity and desolation never disturbed, because she had a deeply rooted and vigorous faith. And thus we read in her *Autobiography* that her falling to sleep after receiving Communion did not disconcert her; neither did that fearful desolation which she had in the last days of her life, when the light of faith appeared to have gone out in her heart.

How many of us, on the other hand, when we go to prayer and experience consolation, come forth content with the assurance that God loves us a great deal? But if we do not feel Him, we come forth broken-hearted, sadly thinking that He has no regard for us, or that we have none for Him. And simply because we do not feel Him!

And yet there are so many things, even material ones, that we do not feel. Do we feel the blood circulating through our arteries? Do we feel the mysterious workings of the brain? Do we notice that marvel by which digested food becomes assimilated and transformed into our proper substance? When we were children and youths, did we feel an increase of growth each day? And if we do not feel these material things, how is it that we wish to feel that which is spiritual?

This light of faith with which we always encounter God is in a certain sense the only way, and in a certain sense it is not. It is the only way, because in this world every manner of knowing God has faith as its basis. If we except the case in which our Lord grants certain extraordinary graces, there is not on this earth any other light by which we can know and contemplate divine things than the light of faith. But in a certain sense it is not the only way, because among the gifts of the Holy Ghost there are at least three which serve to aid faith: the gifts of knowledge, understanding, and wisdom. These gifts do not supplant the light of faith; they merely remove certain imperfections from it and bestow upon it certain prerogatives. They do not take its place; they simply make it more perfect.

One of the proper effects of these gifts is precisely this: under their influence we not only know divine things, but at times we also savor them.

Hence it can be said that through the medium of these gifts, particularly through that of wisdom, we savor God. But it is necessary to understand this expression of the mystics well. It does not mean that we perceive God with our bodily senses. By this expression we manifest as well as we can that conscious knowledge, which is in a certain sense experimental and intuitive, that we have of God, particularly through the gift of wisdom. Even then, however, we perceive God with those two savors of which we spoke: bitter and sweet; honey and myrrh. Who would have believed it, that the most excruciating desolations are the fruits of the Holy Ghost; that these sensations which desolate souls experience and which seem to them to be the very tortures of hell, are produced by the Holy Ghost through the medium of the gifts?

Thus with the gifts of the Holy Ghost one often feels the spiritual life, but in many instances it would be better not to feel it, since it is experienced in a terrible and crucifying manner.

To sum up: the first secret in finding our Lord is faith. He does not hide Himself from the gaze of faith, nor can He elude it. Faith never has obstacles; it penetrates all recesses; it pierces all veils. If only we would understand the secret of living by faith, of going to God by the way of obscure faith!

We approach the tabernacle, and we feel

nothing, just as though we were drawing near an empty tabernacle. We say: "Jesus is here"; but it is as though we were pronouncing words in an unknown language, for they move not a single fiber of our heart. But faith assures us that God is there; and if we would comport ourselves in harmony with what faith tells us, how different our prayer would be! We speak to Jesus, but we do not feel that He is listening to us, nor that He is answering us; and our colloquy languishes, and soon we do not know what to say. But faith tells us that Jesus listens to us and that He speaks to us, and that He needs neither external sounds nor extraordinary means in order to speak with us. He is the divine Master who speaks and instructs without the noise of words. And if faith assures me that Jesus hears me, speaks to me, and loves me, then delights and consolations are not necessary: no, not anything at all.

The obscurity of faith, to be sure, does not accommodate itself to our sensible tastes. We would desire, above all things else, to feel; and faith is not for feeling and savoring, but for knowing.

"I do not find God," you may say. You do not find Him according to your way, that is, in a sensible manner. But do you believe? If you have faith, you already know that God does not stand far from you, because "in Him we live and move and are"; because He surrounds us on the right hand and on the left, above and below; because He penetrates us and lives by grace in the most intimate part of our soul; because He is present in that flower, in that fragrance, in that ray of light, in that glorious sky, everywhere. Consequently, if we knew how to profit from faith and to live by faith, we would always find God, and thus we would have solved our problem, we would have discovered the great secret of the interior life.

5

We have just seen that faith is the means whereby to find our hidden God, and that there are no veils so thick nor darknesses so dense that they hide Him from the eyes of faith. Therefore vivifying our faith, exercising ourselves in it, and accustoming ourselves to live by it, hold such an important place in the spiritual life.

The other means of communicating with God are not continual; but faith is. I know of no soul that has lived in perpetual delights. In the spiritual life days of fervor always alternate with days of aridity, and days of light with days of darkness. Even the state of our own body exerts its influence in this matter, but it is pre-eminently the dispensation of grace which demands that things be this way. Since, therefore, faith never fails us, we can always go to God by means of it; it is the unfailing element of our spiritual life. It is so stable that even mortal sin does not extinguish it; it is a light that always accompanies us during our pilgrimage on earth. If in order to live the interior life we should stand in need of consolations or of extraordinary graces, such as, for example, visions and divine locutions, it would be something very difficult, if not impossible; and, when all is said and done, it would be something intermittent. But none of these things is necessary; the faith that lives continually in our heart is sufficient.

Faith is not only the perpetual element of our spiritual life; it is also a most firm element, firmer by far than consolations and extraordinary graces. St. Peter, after having alluded to the Transfiguration, of which he was a privileged witness, and to that heavenly voice, the voice of the Father, which his own ears heard on the height of Thabor, assures us that, despite everything else, we have something more firm and more secure: "And we have the more firm prophetical word," [6] the revealed word, that is, the faith.

In fact, the faith is something more firm and more secure than would be the appearance of our Lord to us and His speech with us. How often have we thought that if we could see our Lord, as St. Margaret Mary and St. Theresa did, that surely love would be enkindled in our heart and that then we could easily practice all the virtues! Who does not imagine that an apparition would be something most efficacious in the spiritual life! Never-

[6] II Pet. 1:19.

theless, I repeat that the light of faith is more firm and more sure than an apparition.

For be it known that when our Lord appears, He does not come in His proper person; nor does He manifest His proper humanity, but rather something external that makes an impression on our retina, or, what is more common, an interior image that is impressed on our imagination. In every instance there is always the question of whether an apparition is of supernatural origin, or whether it is something diabolic, or whether it is an outright hallucination. And if all signs and opinions concerning that apparition or locution point to a supernatural origin, in all cases one can have no more than moral certitude; whereas faith gives us absolute certitude. Faith is more firm and sure than all apparitions and words and extraordinary locutions: "And we have the more firm prophetical word."

I recall a person who arrived at a very high degree of prayer by means of this very simple procedure. She said to herself: "If I should see our Lord, how would I react? What would I say to Him? How would I comport myself with Him?" Then she would vivify her faith and say: "I do not see Him with my eyes, but faith assures me that He is present in the tabernacle. Now, if He is here before me, I wish to enact what I should feel and say and do, as I would feel and say and do it if I were seeing Him with my bodily eyes." Thus she intensified her faith and facilitated her intercourse with God.

We, on the other hand, often keep seeking for sensible and pleasant experiences, and we keep wishing for ease and satisfaction in our communications with God; we long for that special light, that divine impression which at times brings us close to God. There is no doubt that we should not refuse those graces if God accords them to us; but we ought not to seek after them nor yearn anxiously for them nor attach ourselves to them.

Can we make our prayer with ease? Then let us be transported with it. Is our soul flooded with light? Then let us profit from it that our heart may glow. At the present time, however, do we lack all this? Then let us not be disturbed, for faith should suffice us in such a way that we should comport ourselves today as we comported ourselves yesterday. Yesterday we loved God in light and in joy; today let us love Him in darkness and spiritual dryness. If we had the surety of His love yesterday, we ought also to have it today. His love does not depend on the changes of our heart, nor does it alter because our sensible dispositions change. His love is everlastingly the same.

We have marvelous examples of this in the lives of the saints, especially in that of St. Theresa of Jesus, who lived many years in terrible desolation, with no other light to guide her in her spiritual life than the light of faith. St. Theresa of the Child

Jesus also passed almost her whole life desolate and disconsolate, not to speak of that terrible darkness of the final years.

Let us resolve, then, to live by faith, and let us not presume to mark out for our Lord the way He must follow with respect to our souls; rather let us be well disposed to receive from His hand whatever may come. Let us put away, once and for all, the erroneous manner of evaluating our spiritual life by the way we feel; that is, judging that when we feel elated, we are in a good state, and that when we do not feel elated we are in a bad state. No. The state of our soul does not depend on our feelings. Sensible joy is a gratuity; it is of secondary importance. That which is constant, firm, and sure is faith.

Much less ought we to judge God according to our feelings, as though the love of God were so fickle and inconstant that it depended on the changeableness and inconstancy of our emotions. No. The love of God is constant, unchangeable, eternal. In spite of our faults, miseries, and sins, God does not cease to love us. With greater reason, then, does He continue loving us in periods of spiritual dryness, despite the unfeeling state of our heart. Faith assures us of this. Often we have this thought: God is cold or indifferent toward me. And in reality it is I that am indifferent and cold; yet I try to judge God in accordance with the state in which I find myself. And in truth, despite my coldness and indifference, true and solid fervor is not wanting to me. The proof is in the fact that I suffer, thinking that God is treating me with indifference. If I did not love Him, I would not suffer because of it, since the indifference of a person for whom I do not care causes me no concern.

Various souls are ingenious in tormenting themselves, thinking that if they do not feel God sensibly, they are being punished because of this or that infidelity. "I denied our Lord this sacrifice," they say; "I committed that fault; I was not generous on that occasion; because of this fault God is justly punishing me, taking from me sensible fervor." No doubt, from time to time God can punish our failings, depriving us of some spiritual thing. But let it be well understood that this does not always occur. Moreover, even when He chastises us, faith assures us that He does not cease to love us. Yes, even more can be said: it is precisely because He loves us that He chastises us; His chastisements are proofs of His love. "Whom the Lord loveth, He chastiseth." [7] God corrects and chastises those He loves, just as a tender and loving father corrects and chastises his sons precisely because he loves them and desires their true welfare.

This criterion of judging the state of our soul by our feelings is very erroneous; for we usually

[7] Prov. 3:12.

are better or worse than we think. There is no one that enjoys consolation who does not feel that he is almost a saint. This is so because sensible consolations, especially when they have a certain intensity, calm the passions, rest the soul, and make the doing of good so easy that they give us the feeling of holiness. The truth is that our feelings do not reveal the true state of our soul: we feel that we are better than we really are.

On the other hand, when spiritual dryness and helplessness come, when the passions rise up, and when the doing of all good becomes almost impossible, when temptations rock us, and our inclinations to evil become quickened, we believe that we are almost demons, or at the least that we have fallen back and are doing badly. In these instances our feelings do not manifest to us in a truthful way the state of our soul: we are really less wicked than we feel. Let us judge with a superior criterion, with that of faith. With faith we can always and in all circumstances enter into communication with God, and we can have a more exact knowledge of the true state of our soul.

One can still make this objection to me: faith is truly the great means whereby to find God, but what is one to do when it is precisely the faith that is wanting to us? At times, since it appears to lose all its force and all its efficacy, we are not able to make an act of faith. The words indeed come from our lips, but we do not perceive that they spring from the heart. On other occasions, even more trying, it seems that we have positively lost the faith; everything that faith teaches seems to us an illusion, and the whole supernatural world fades away, and only this material and gross world remains to us. But all this is only apparent, and in the designs of God it has as its purpose the sharpening and perfecting of our faith.

The normal means that God uses to implant and to develop a virtue in us is by permitting attacks and temptations against it. Hence, when God permits us to be tempted in any field, He does so that the virtue which is assaulted may develop and become perfect.

This is a truth that is not easy to admit, since we hold to the belief that temptations are for the purpose of destroying virtues. But this is not so; God permits them only that virtues may increase. Hence when God wishes that a person should distinguish himself in any virtue, He increases attacks and unlooses terrible and persistent temptations against that virtue.[8]

Consequently, when faith suffers great temptations, when doubts torment us, when an icy indifference takes hold of us, and when we feel everything sinking from under us, all this means that our Lord needs to exercise us in a special

[8] Evidently the temptations under discussion are those that God permits, not those that a soul seeks through its own imprudences, such as exposing itself to voluntary and dangerous occasions of sin.

way in the faith in order that it may become more deeply rooted, more intense, in order, perhaps, that it may become heroic. We feel that we have no faith, and yet we have it; it seems that we have lost it, and yet this is not true; for our faith is passing through a crystal, from which it will come forth more pure and more brilliant. It seems that our acts of faith come only from our lips, and yet this is not true; for in the depth of our heart we believe, and those acts of faith made in the midst of darkness, of struggles, and of temptations are more vigorous and serve to implant that virtue more strongly.

This exercise of faith must not be intermittent, but continual, just as continual as the spiritual life. Thus just as the life of the body undergoes no interruption, since whether asleep or awake, working or resting, we are ever living—and our lungs breathe, and our heart beats, and our blood circulates, for the interruption of life would necessarily be death—in the same way the interior life must never be interrupted. We must always be in union with God by means of faith. Relations with the neighbor can indeed be interrupted; there are times for dealing with him, and times for being alone. But the spiritual life and our relations with God must ever be continuous. Close to or far away from the tabernacle, in our exercises of piety or in our work, alone or dealing with the neighbor, we must always be with God.

And for this continuous interior life faith is indispensable. If we should have this virtue living in us, we would find God everywhere: in church, on the street, in the home, at the office, in the workshop, at the factory, in the commotion of the city and in the quiet of the country. For faith encounters God wherever He is; and God is everywhere.

There is no question of living two lives, one imposed upon the other: the ordinary life and the spiritual life. No. We must live only one life, the life of faith, which should permeate, transform, and unite with our ordinary life in such a way that the two form but one single life. Persons are, as it were, stairs by which to ascend to God; all creation is His revelation, and we are able to find Him in every creature.

There are people who speak thus: "Today I began my spiritual life well, but such and such a one came along and made me forget about God, and then everything was lost." But if such and such a person discloses God to me? If what he tells me is, in one way or other, a divine message? How can it be possible that the messengers of the Beloved make me forget about Him? All creatures, even those that are annoying and importunate, are divine messengers. The trouble is that we see them through human eyes. If we would only see them through the eyes of faith!

The same thing happens to us that occurs with

people that use two kinds of glasses, one for see-ing close at hand and the other for seeing at a distance. Thus we at times and for certain matters use the glasses of faith; and at other times and for other matters we use the glasses of poor human reason. How many things, when they are seen with the spectacles of reason, astonish and discon-cert us! If we would always use the spectacles of faith, nothing would disturb us, nothing would be capable of breaking off our relations with God; we would find Him everywhere and in every creature, since faith discovers and encounters Him everywhere and in all things.

6

Let us see now how in the interior life "the ways of God are not our ways." With this in view we shall finish the solution of our problem. We con-ceive the spiritual life according to our own way of thinking: that is, in a very human way, espe-cially in the beginning when we have as yet no experience with it. We imagine that it is a life that always tends upward, in which a person continually ascends and never falls back. And we neglect to consider that the spiritual life, as all human life, must have its peaks and its low points. We think that each day our faults should keep vanishing and that our soul should continue to be purified without cease. And indeed our soul does continue to be purified more and more each day, but this purification is one of faith; it is not a tangible purification that we can perceive as in the case of our findings in the particular examination of conscience, when we note, for example, that yesterday we had eight faults, today six, tomorrow four, and the day after none.

We think that the spiritual life is one of ever-growing fervor, in which we feel ourselves more enthusiastic, more closely united to our Lord, each day. We imagine the spiritual life to be a way of light, without eclipses, not one whit different from what occurs with the days of nature: first there is the softness of the aurora, then the dawn filled with its hopes; next comes the sun filling the earth little by little with its heat and its light until the fullness of noonday is at hand. This is how we picture the spiritual life. Temptations? Assuredly they will come, but they will be as spiritual diversions to break the monotony of life; and naturally they will be temptations that will always be overcome.

But the ways of God are not our ways. I almost dare to say that the spiritual life is almost the contrary of what we fancy it. It is true that it goes upward, but by our lowering ourselves. It is true that it purifies the soul, but in the midst of temptations and falls. It is true that its light increases, yet the light is one that is overshadowed with darkness. Therefore, that the light may increase, the darkness must envelop us; that the purification may continue, the most painful temptations must besiege us; and that true fervor may take root in the soul, sensible fervor must frequently forsake us. Thus in the midst of darkness, of helplessness, of struggles, of temptations, of falls, we continue going upward; yet we do not notice that we are ascending until we arrive at the goal of our aspirations.

The ignorance of this truth, that the ways of God are very different from our ways, is the cause of much confusion for the soul. Every time we suffer a calamity in our spiritual life, we grow alarmed and think we have lost our way. For we have fancied an even road for ourselves, a footpath, a way strewn with flowers. Hence upon finding ourselves in a rough way, one filled with thorns, one lacking all attraction, we think we have lost the road; whereas it is only that the ways of God are very different from our ways.

Sometimes the biographies of the saints tend to foster this illusion; that is, when they do not fully reveal the profound story of those souls, or when they disclose it only in a fragmentary manner, selecting solely the attractive and pleasing features. They call our attention to the hours that the saints spent in prayer, to the generosity with which they practiced virtue, to the consolations they received from God. We see only what is shining and beautiful, and we lose sight of the struggles, darknesses, temptations, and falls through which they passed. And we think like this: Oh, if I could live as those souls! What peace, what light, what love was theirs! Yes, that is what we see; but if we would look deeply into the hearts of the saints, we would understand that the ways of God are not our ways.

The ways of God for attaining perfection are ways of struggle, of dryness, of humiliations, and even of falls.

To be sure, there is light and peace and sweetness in the spiritual life: and indeed a splendid light before which the doctrine of the most learned men of earth is darkness, a peace above anything that could be desired, and a sweetness that surpasses all the consolations of earth. There is all this, but all in its proper time; and in each instance it is something transient. What is usual and most common in the spiritual life are those periods in which we are compelled to suffer, and which disconcert us because we were expecting something different. Most souls that live in the midst of temptations think they are doing poorly; those that have the misfortune to fall believe all is lost; those that live in desolations fancy it is their fault that God has forsaken them. Therefore it is most important in the spiritual life to realize that we are not lost when we travel those strange roads; we need only realize that they are God's ways, that it will cost us much effort to walk them, and that we shall need much abnegation to travel them. Yet they are the true ways to attain perfection.

In a particular way the chief difficulty by which most souls are held back is desolation. Temptations and falls are in a special manner the stumbling blocks of the active life, whereas desolation is apparently the great difficulty of the contemplative life. Hence we could say that the great secret of the spiritual life consists in knowing how to value desolations, in knowing how to profit from them.

There is no doubt that we must also know how to use divine consolations. For there are souls that are too austere, that grow terrified when consolations come, and that do not wish them, just as there are others that cling to them inordinately, seeking them for their own sake. We ought to receive with gratitude from the hands of God whatever He gives us, consolations as well as desolations. Both come from God to effect a divine work in our souls.

But not much is necessary to profit from consolations, nor do they usually give us difficulty; and if we cling to them, God will take care to remove them from us. The danger lies in desolations because they trouble us, because it is rarely and with difficulty that we know how to profit from them. We take it for granted that the dark nights are not very frequent in the interior life; but

aridities are one of the most frequent occurrences
in every spiritual life. Often the sky becomes overcast, our facility for prayer vanishes, and our soul
feels an utter powerlessness. It cannot meditate or
form affective acts; it cannot even remain thinking
on the same thing for two consecutive moments.
At other times there is, as it were, a habitual dissipation: the soul passes unceasingly, like a butter-
fly, from one affair to another, and in a moment
it flits over a frightening multitude of things.

How much effort prayer costs then! It seems
eternal. When the soul enjoys sweetness the hours
seem to it to be seconds, and it wonders how they
passed so quickly. Thus are the periods of gladness, moments that quickly pass. On the other
hand, those of sorrow are never-ending; they seem
to be centuries. Thus does the time of prayer
seem to the soul in aridity. The soul looks at the
clock, thinking that surely the hour has already
passed, whereas only five minutes have elapsed.
Then it becomes alarmed, does not know what to
think, does not know how to comport itself in
that situation. It decides that everything is lost,
and thinks it bears the fault that God has forsaken
it. And then one of two things happens: either
it despairs, suffering terribly, or it gives up prayer,
thinking there is no other solution to its difficulty.

And if it cannot give up prayer, it goes to it
because it has to; but it allows its mind to wander
freely wheresoever it will, or it tries to fight against

its aridity, but without knowing how, and very often the soul increases its own torment by wearying its spirit and making its situation worse.

When shall we convince ourselves that "the ways of God are not our ways," and that these paths that are so full of darkness are the ones that lead to divine union?

But you may object. "How strange these ways are!" They appear strange to us because of our dullness, but they are precious. In the spiritual life desolations have a special beauty. This is true, of course, when they are seen in other souls, because when we have them in our own we lack the serenity necessary to know how to appreciate them. A desolation is beautiful in the same sense that the ocean is beautiful when it is agitated by a tremendous storm, or as the desert is beautiful in its aridity and its silence, or as those volcanic areas are beautiful where in all directions nothing is seen except capricious rock formations, deep gulleys, and absolute barrenness of vegetation. Thus, surely, is a desolate soul beautiful in the eyes of God. This is tragic beauty, dramatic by its contrasts: on one hand, our misery and our littleness are made manifest; on the other, our fidelity to God is made to stand out, that fidelity which on no account abandons its service and which continues true in its march toward God.

In their tragedies the Greeks always depicted a great character, a heroic figure who contended against destiny, and who in the midst of trials and fearful dangers remained unmoved and thus succeeded in triumphing. Such is the tragedy of desolation: a weak, powerless, hapless soul battles in the midst of a thousand difficulties and dangers, yet despite everything it remains tranquil and conquers in the end. It is like Jacob contending with the angel, that is, contending with the Lord. Because of this, God changed Jacob's name to Israel, which means "strong against God." In desolation we struggle against the Most High and, although we are fragile creatures, we are "strong against God." It is like Christ agonizing in Gethsemane, or painfully climbing the hill of Calvary, or dying nailed to a cross. To the eyes of human reason this is an ignominy, but to the eyes of faith it has a tragic and sublime beauty.

The spiritual advantages that desolations bring us are so many and of such a nature that, if the desolations did not exist, we would have to invent them. No one has been sanctified without experiencing them. And in what large measures! St. Theresa of Jesus endured them for eighteen years. St. Magdalen de Pazzi, for twenty-two. What lengthy sacrifices our Lord demands! He who fared best was St. Francis of Assisi; for with ingenuous tenderness he persisted with God, and thus he endured terrible desolations for only two years.

In order that the soul may attain perfection it

must be despoiled of all, as we have already seen: not only of external and material things, but also of those that are internal and spiritual. But how can we be despoiled of spiritual things except through the medium of desolations?

It is easy to see how we can rid ourselves of material things. If I have an attachment to money, I can give it away; if I cling to the good opinion of others, I can seek humiliations. But how can we deliver ourselves from spiritual things, if God does not remove that which is enticing in them through desolations? And that is precisely what God does in periods of dryness: He does not deprive us of His grace or of His gifts, but only of the pleasing elements that they possess. When the soul is desolate, to what can it cling? This is one of the purposes of desolations: to despoil us of spiritual attachments; and there is no other means but desolations by which to do this.

Furthermore, to achieve the contemplative life one must live by faith in all its fullness. But to effect this, God needs to place us in those critical states in which there remains nothing to us but faith; for in the midst of consolations we have no need to make those acts of faith which are more intense, lively, profound, even heroic. On pleasant days it seems that we do not even need faith, so clear do divine things appear to us. There is no doubt that even in the midst of consolations faith is fundamentally present, but we have no occasion to exercise it heroically as in times of desolation. In fair weather the voyager has no concern about a life-preserver, whereas the shipwrecked person grasps for it frantically.

7

Another advantage of spiritual dryness is that it produces a deep and true humility in us. When we hear a sermon on humility, or read a spiritual treatise, or meditate seriously, we come to the conclusion that we are very miserable beings. But this conviction is no more than theoretical. When we are told that there are torrid regions in Africa, and that the temperature is oppressive, and that traveling is difficult and painful in those desert areas, we form some idea of those torrid climates. But what a difference there is in hearing about all this and in going there and suffering from the heat and feeling all its effects in our body!

The same thing occurs with humility. To be given theoretical knowledge of our misery is quite different from feeling it, coming in contact with it, and knowing it by experience. And in desolations we feel our helplessness and misery in such a way that when we have thus perceived it we never forget it.

When peace returns to souls that have passed through desolation, and when our Lord pours out special graces upon them, they receive them with gratitude and love; but they do not raise their head; they are mindful of their misery; it remains impressed upon them to such an extent that there is no fear that they will become proud over divine favors. This is true because in time of trial we feel our misery; in that period we know by experience that we are not capable of a good thought. When we read about this in St. Paul, we are inclined to think that it is an exaggeration of the saint. But no; desolation shows us truly that we are incapable of having a good thought or a pious affection; and thus we understand the truth of what the Apostle says.

Ordinarily we give vent to sentiments like this: "If love is to our soul what air is to our lungs, what can be easier than to love our Lord?" But in time of trial we are not capable of making an act of love, no matter how hard we wish to. Then there is so much dissipation of mind that even the most insignificant thing distracts, no matter how serious our nature may be: the slightest noise, a fly that swirls around, the opening of a door, a person passing by—anything whatever distracts us as though we were the veriest children. Is not this to feel our own miserable state?

Furthermore, with desolation come struggles and temptations; and the worst feelings well up in our heart. At such a time the soul thinks: "My life has been a deception; I thought I had achieved some virtue; I thought I knew how to pray. But

I have accomplished nothing; all is a deception; for me all is lost." Is not this to realize our miserable condition? What a difference between describing it and feeling it! In this way desolations exercise us in the life of faith; they detach us from the spiritual gifts of God, and they produce in us a deep understanding of ourselves, a great fund of humility. Are not these great advantages enough for us to come to an appreciation of desolation? How could we ever obtain them by means of consolations in that pleasant and easy life we dreamed of? Let us, therefore, be reconciled to trials, since they are a most important factor in the spiritual life: they have their beauty; they are fruitful; and they possess incomparable advantages. Ordinarily speaking, we ought not to pray for them, because perhaps this would be asking amiss; but we surely ought to accept them with gratitude when God sends them to us.

Spiritual dryness also exercises us in another important virtue, patience. Whoever has felt desolation knows to what an extent it makes us practice this virtue. Patience is of three types: patience with God, with ourselves, and with our neighbor. Of these three classes of patience, the first two are the hardest and precisely the ones that are exercised in time of trial. In it our Lord is the one who immolates us, and we need much patience that we may submit to being treated as He wills with us. And much patience with ourselves is also needed to remain faithful and firm in a period of desolation.

It is no little advantage to us to be exercised in patience in this way, for Sacred Scripture says that patience produces a perfect work: "My brethren, count it all joy when you shall fall into divers temptations; knowing that the trying of your faith worketh patience. And patience hath a perfect work." [9] All this is applied in a special way to desolation, which is one of the greatest trials we can undergo.

And in the beatitudes that our Lord teaches us in the Sermon on the Mount, the eighth, which is the consummation and the epitome of all the others, is the beatitude of patience. Hence patience, which is nothing else than tenacious perseverance in good, is what takes us to the height of perfection, the supreme happiness of earth and the prelude to the blessedness of heaven.

To pass months and years with dryness of spirit, with helplessness of soul, with turbulence of passions, in continual darkness, and, notwithstanding, to remain generously faithful to God—this is

---

[9] Jas. 1:2–4. It is to be noted, however, that the Greek text does not use the indicative, but the optative, which would change the meaning not a little. It could then be translated: "May patience accompany the perfect work." The Apostle James understands for "perfect work," *opus perfectum;* that is, the spiritual activity which fully accomplishes the designs of God upon a soul. At any rate the authority of the Latin text remains intact, and the doctrine that is deduced from it is true.

something heroic which greatly pleases our Lord and effects the perfect work in our souls. We cannot arrive at perfection if we do not pass through tribulations.

There are still other and more important advantages than the foregoing ones. Desolations refine the love that is within us. When dryness comes to us, we immediately believe we are losing love, since with our narrow outlook we reason as follows: "I do not feel that I love; therefore I do not love." And then we yearn for the days of consolation when we fancied that the sun of love truly lighted up the heaven of our soul. And if desolation grows stronger, we arrive at the stage where we perceive not only that we do not feel love but also that we are annoyed and disgusted by all spiritual things. How are we going to believe that we love when our heart is agitated by such feelings?

But we are mistaken. Love like gold needs purification, and this is what is going on within us. A thing is said to be pure when it contains no admixture of any other thing: that is pure water which is not mixed with anything else, which contains nothing that is foreign to the nature of water. That is pure love which contains no foreign element. And that foreign element can be nothing else than self-love. To purify love, then, is to remove from it all self-love. Various methods are used to purify substances: some are passed through a filter, others are distilled, and still others, such as gold, are purified by fire. Love is purified by making it pass through the crucible of desolation.

In times of consolation when we go to prayer with pleasure, when we place ourselves immediately in the presence of God, and when everything goes smoothly, there is no question about our seeking Him and about our giving pleasure to Him. But we cannot deny that we also are going to give pleasure to ourselves. It is so sweet to be with Jesus in the hours of consolation. Such is the delight suffusing our soul that we could spend hours in His presence, most assuredly because we love Him, but also because we are receiving delight. That love is not entirely pure.

In times of trial a soul that is faithful to God makes the same prayer as when it is enjoying consolation. Why does it do so? Does it go to it to seek self? Or what does it seek if it encounters nothing? The soul well knows that the prayer period is a time of torture, and yet it goes to it, as St. Lawrence went to the grill, in order that the fire of desolation might consume it. Its only reason for going could be to please God. It is like St. Theresa of the Little Flower, who did not worry about her dryness in prayer, considering that she did not go to it to please herself but only God. Behold the purity of love that is achieved only in affliction.

But all this is nothing more than the surface; there is a divine richness in spiritual dryness that produces a marvelous transformation in the soul. St. Theresa of the Child Jesus tells us of it in her *Autobiography,* but with such ingenuousness that she disconcerts us, and we do not suspect that she encloses so profound a teaching in such simple words.

A case in point is that in which the saint tells us that she did not grow alarmed when she drowsed after Holy Communion, since she reflected that children are just as pleasing to their parents when they are asleep as when they are awake. Moreover, as she adds, doctors induce sleep in their patients for certain operations. How true it is that in the spiritual order there are certain operations for which it is necessary to anesthetize souls! Why is it necessary to give an anesthetic to sick people? Without doubt it is in order that they may not suffer; but above everything else it is that they may not cause trouble. There are people of great endurance who would be able to undergo an operation without an anesthetic. Nevertheless the surgeon anesthetizes them, since every movement of a patient, even though involuntary, can ruin certain very delicate operations.

Similarly there are operations in the supernatural order in which we work with our Lord and cooperate with Him in them. But there are others of a very intimate nature in which the one thing

He asks of us is that we do not hinder Him; and in order that we do not impede Him He gives us a spiritual anesthetic; that is, desolation, since it is a kind of paralysis of the spirit which renders us helpless.

In time of spiritual dryness souls often think as follows: "I go to prayer and I do nothing, absolutely nothing." The soul does nothing, but God does a great deal, although the soul may not be aware of His secret and mysterious operations. But when the period of trial passes, we find that we are different. Without our knowing how or when, a profound change was wrought in us: our love is more solid; our virtue has become stronger. According to the familiar expression, we have come out of the trial "as new." What does it matter that those afflictions may endure for years on end, if finally the soul emerges as new, fit to be united with God and to realize fully the role it was destined to fill on earth?

Desolation, then, is the indispensable means whereby the soul attains its transformation into Jesus, the supreme goal and the perfection of holiness.

We think, perhaps, that transformation into Jesus is something that we can achieve with God's help. But no; simply having God's help is not sufficient. God alone can accomplish it; and the only help that we can give Him is to allow Him a free hand, not to impede Him.

We could conceive that the method for transforming us into Jesus would be this: The Gospel has left us a perfect representation of Jesus, precise indications of His moral make-up; hence I need do nothing more than continue imitating Him little by little. I have so many years to become meek, so many to become humble, so many to become obedient, and so on. Thus I need only continue imitating Him virtue by virtue, availing myself of ascetical helps such as the particular examination, meditation, spiritual reading.

When in this way, after much time and labor, I have copied the lineaments of Jesus, I shall be but a sketch, an outline; I shall possess something similar to Him, but I shall not be that living representation which is necessary for transformation. Transformation requires that God Himself come to work in the soul and, so to speak, make us anew. Hence in Ezechiel, God says that He will take away from us our stony heart and give us a new heart and a new spirit.[10]

Do not think that these are hyperboles, divine exaggerations. No. On the contrary, the reality goes much beyond symbols. Truly, when a soul has been transformed, it has a new way of seeing, feeling, and operating. Hence this transformation cannot be achieved by our poor human efforts;

[10] Ezech. 11:19. "And I will give them one heart, and will put a new spirit in their bowels: and I will take away the stony heart out of their flesh, and will give them a heart of flesh."

God must come and work in the deepest recesses of our being; and, that we may not hinder Him, He anesthetizes us by means of spiritual desolation. Therefore, when a soul has passed through the great trials of the spiritual life, it stands on the threshold of union, of transformation into Jesus.

We appreciate, then, the value of spiritual affliction. It will be painful and hard, but it is of the utmost value and altogether necessary for arriving at sanctity. I know of only one exception: the Blessed Virgin. Since she was perfect from the moment of her Immaculate Conception, she had no need of desolations to attain sanctity. Nevertheless, no one has suffered more terrible afflictions than she did in the years of her exile after the death and ascension of her Son. But there is this difference: she did not need those desolations for her sanctification, though through them she grew in holiness. By them, in union with her Son, she procured graces for us and fulfilled her role of co-redeemer and mother of all men.

We must make our choice. Either we choose transformation, and then we also accept the desolation without which it cannot be arrived at; or we refuse desolation, and then we must also reject transformation and thus give ourselves over to dragging out our life in a common mediocrity.

Desolation is a cross, but one of the most precious, one of the most divine. It is not wrought by the hand of men, but by God Himself; it is a

work of the Holy Ghost. The trial, therefore, is
made in accordance with the measure of each
soul, perfectly fitted to its circumstances, require-
ments, and mission, and to the degree of perfection to which God has destined it. Hence trial
possesses an eminently sanctifying power. Let us
open our arms to it, then, and salute it with the
same cry as the Church uses: "Hail, O cross, our
only hope!" In this way, by reason of all that has
been said concerning spiritual afflictions, this truth
is once more established: God's ways are not our
ways.

8

I trust that we now have a better realization
of the worth of spiritual trials, and that consequently we have come to a better understanding
of the importance they hold in the spiritual life.
But it is not sufficient to understand and to appreciate them; we must know how to profit from
them. This is the final matter that I am going to
treat of.

I must remark, however, that desolations, like
all crosses (although desolations have a special
efficacy), are profitable to us, even during the
times when we do not correspond perfectly to the
action that God exercises in our souls by means
of them. For the cross always possesses the power
to bestow good, even when ungraciously borne,

unless, of course, we openly reject it. Have we not observed in souls that have withdrawn from God, how, when they have a great sorrow, grief is always fruitful for them, even though they do not know how to profit from it fully by receiving it as virtuous souls do? Many persons return to God and become converted because of a disappointment, a sickness, a humiliation. This is so because the cross is most efficacious, and it does us good even when we drag it along. Yet we may logically affirm that, to the extent that we avail ourselves of it and correspond to the designs of God in sending it to us, to that extent will the cross have greater sanctifying power.

We can enumerate various categories corresponding to the different attitudes of the soul toward the cross and, at the same time, to the profit the soul draws from it. Some persons reject the cross openly, and it profits them nothing. Others, after some delay, take it up, and then it begins to do them good. Others accept it, and thus it is more profitable to them. Lastly, there are others who not only accept it, but also love it and seek it; and unquestionably for them it is profitable to the highest degree. Let us see, then, how we ought to make use of desolations, and how we ought to conduct our soul during them.

In the first place, to profit from a cross we must, before all things else, recognize it. It seems strange to say that we ought to realize that we have a cross. Can we be unaware that we are suffering if we feel our sufferings? There is no question that when we bear the cross on our shoulders we are aware that we are undergoing pain; but very many times we do not advert to the fact that this is a cross, since we do not think that all suffering is a cross in the sense that whenever we suffer we carry a cross on our shoulders. But all suffering, no matter whence it comes, is a cross, and consequently it leads us to God and is fruitful for our souls. Not only the sufferings that God sends us directly, but also those that come from creatures, the devil, or ourselves, are crosses.

Let us suppose that a soul is suffering the consequences of its own faults. Are these consequences a cross? Are they helpful in bringing the soul to God? Unquestionably. The soul did wrong when it gave rise to these consequences; but it does well when it embraces them in order to go to God. Hence, to a certain extent, the desire to know whether or not we bear the blame in what we suffer is foolish questioning. How many souls are disconcerted because of this attitude! When they suffer anything, they say to themselves: "This is not a cross; this is not a spiritual affliction." Let us suppose the statement is true; that I am in the wrong for having brought about that state of affairs. But now that I am in this painful situation, can I not use it to sanctify myself?

We are to blame for the cross of Jesus Christ

with which He redeemed us. Of what is the cross of Christ wrought? Of sins. The cross of our Lord has a deadly origin; and, notwithstanding this, it is the source of our redemption, since Jesus sanctified it and offered His sacrifice on it. It was precisely the cross that aided Him in redeeming us from the very sins that are responsible for it. Thus I am able to turn the very consequences of my sins into an instrument of health and of life. If the state of my soul is the result of my failings, I can, if I endure it as I ought, bring about its conversion into a fountain of life for me.

Thus, in a certain sense, the cause of our afflictions matters little. In all instances we ought to see in them a cross, and we ought to make use of them for our sanctification. If it is a punishment, well, punishments are fruitful in this life. In the next, the eternal punishment of hell does not have this fruitfulness; yet even from the depth of hell the glory of God is manifest. Hell is not fruitful for the damned, but it is for God since it renders glory to Him. The chastisements of earth also give glory to God, but at the same time they are fruitful for our souls.

It matters little, then, whether our affliction is a punishment or a grace from God, the consequence of our sins or a gift from heaven; in all instances it is a cross, and we can turn it to account for our sanctification. Thus, if we view our suffer-

ings and the state of our soul with the spirit of
faith, we must see a cross in them; and from the
moment that we view them in that light we transform them.

To regard our present affliction as an abandonment by God or as a great fault in our soul is very
different from regarding it as a cross, that is, as
a means leading us to God. Hence the first thing
we must do to use desolation well is to consider
it a cross, to view it with the eyes of faith. And
this attitude is most important, since one of the
reasons why we do not profit as we ought from
desolations is that we do not look upon them with
a supernatural regard: we are not correct in our
appraisal of them.

How many souls think in times of desolation,
as I have so often said, that all is lost, and that
their spiritual life has gone to ruin! Invariably the
exact opposite is the real truth. Is the soul aban-
doned by God when our Savior presents it with
the cross? Is a life ruined when the soul walks
the ways of Calvary, which are the paths of redemption? Despite all these considerations on the
excellence of desolations, it is certain that at the
time they occur everything becomes clouded, and
then no human power can make us understand
that the trial through which we are passing is an
exceptional grace from God. If in those moments
we should come to see with clarity the value of

desolation, perhaps we might even cease to suffer, and then desolation itself would lose, at least to a great extent, its efficacy and worth.

But if at the very time of desolation we cannot appreciate it at its full worth, at least the possession of the knowledge just mentioned will serve to implant in the depth of our soul a certain conviction and hope which will give peace and tranquillity, although they may be only in the innermost recesses of our spirit. We shall not appreciate to the full the excellence of desolation and the love that it signifies on the part of God. But at least we shall retain in the depths of our soul the conviction that it is God who is working within us.

But perhaps the following objection will be made. "If I knew that what I am enduring is a true spiritual abandonment, even though this knowledge would not console me fully, still those considerations on its excellence and usefulness would be a source of strength for me. But that is exactly the difficulty. How can it be known that what I am suffering is truly a spiritual desolation?" It can be known through the spiritual director. He can tell us whether or not it is a desolation. Hence the spirit of faith is sufficient for us to see in the word of the priest the word of God, and to submit our own judgment to the judgment of him who represents God in a special manner with respect to our soul.

But unfortunately that spirit of faith is wanting, since we wish to see, feel, and understand by ourselves; and in the hour of desolation we neither see nor feel nor understand. The only thing we see clearly and feel and understand is our own misery and helplessness. At all times, but especially in the hour of desolation, we must have faith and believe that what the minister of God tells us is the truth, even though it should be the most difficult thing to believe. "My director tells me that this is desolation, and therefore desolation it must be."

And if we should not have at hand a spiritual director who knows our soul intimately, what can we do then? The answer has already been given. We do not need to know whether or not what we are undergoing is an affliction that comes directly from God. The attitude that we should take in the one instance is almost the same as in the other. Hence if we ought to comport ourselves in the same manner, why waste time and rack our brains in trying to find out the origin of the trial we are suffering? Let us do what we have to do, and let that be an end to it.

Undoubtedly there can be various special kinds of affliction of divine origin, and in these cases we shall have to wait till the director diagnoses the matter.

To live the interior life with constancy we must bear up well not only with spiritual dryness, but also with everything that God sends us. If I put emphasis on desolations of divine origin, that is because in this matter greater light and strength are necessary to receive them well.

In general the secret of the spiritual life consists in this, that we try, with a spirit of faith and with sincerity of heart, to unite ourselves to God in the midst of all the vicissitudes of life. The important thing is that we withdraw our interior life from that region where the changes and fluctuations of this world shake and disturb it, and place it in that serene region where there are no vacillations, but only stability and peace. Thus the Church petitions in one of her prayers: "That amid the changing things of this world, our hearts may be set where true joy is found." [11]

I am going to explain my thought. When I am filled with spiritual consolations, I should live the spiritual life; when spiritual consolations forsake me, I should continue living the spiritual life. When I have light, I shall live the interior life in light; if I am in darkness, I shall live the interior life in darkness. When God draws near to me, I shall live the spiritual life, perceiving that God is very near to my soul; when God withdraws from me, I shall live the spiritual life without anything or anyone impeding it.

Hence it is not important that we know whether the desolation is this kind or that, but that we live

[11] Collect for the Fourth Sunday after Easter.

the spiritual life in this condition in which we find ourselves. Whether our desolation comes from sickness or from our passions or from God or from the demon or from ourselves matters little. What we must do is not to leave off living the spiritual life in the circumstances in which we are, no matter what may be their origin. Therefore the best rule for the spiritual life is this: To receive moment by moment whatever God sends us and to persevere at all cost with our soul united to God in spite of all vicissitudes. I need not search out anxiously the origin of my state or seek to ascertain whether my condition possesses all the characteristics that are proper to desolation. Whether I have desolation or consolation or anything else, the important thing is to know how to accommodate myself to all these states and how to maintain my union with God in all of them.

Our life is so complex! So very many elements enter into it! We are affected by everything, even by the weather: cold, heat, cloudy days. Hence with greater reason do these various states of our soul affect our being. This fact is especially true in the supernatural order, since God affects us with the most varied invitations of grace, and the devil with his ceaseless solicitations to evil. Again I say: this is the reason why our life is so complex.

Therefore, the wise course is not to analyze those states, but to withdraw our spiritual life from them in order that nothing and nobody may rob us of our treasure, as St. Paul said: "For I am sure that neither death nor life nor angels nor principalities nor powers nor things present nor things to come nor might nor height nor depth nor any other creature shall be able to separate us from the love of God, which is in Christ Jesus our Lord." [12] Let us learn how to guard our treasure equally well at midnight and at high noon, whether the tempest is unleashed, or the sun shines brilliantly in a cloudless sky.

How can we succeed in withdrawing our spiritual life from the changes of time? First of all by faith. Faith is not subject to changes; we have faith always; it is our safest and most unfailing guide. Beyond faith is love: not sensible love, but sure, solid love which is ready to unite us to God in spite of every adverse circumstance. If we possess God by means of faith and of love, the changes of this life matter little. Whatever they may be, we shall continue to live the interior life.

Allow me to make a comparison even though it may appear somewhat prosaic. In all the circumstances of our life, we eat. Poor or rich, joyful or sorrowful, we must eat since it is an indispensable requirement of our nature. The rich dine on exquisite fare, the poor have simple and humble dishes; the joyful eat with gladness, the sorrowful moisten their bread with their tears: but all eat. We find a like truth in the supernatural order.

[12] Rom. 8:38 f.

The food of the soul is the interior life, since God is our life, and to be united to Him is to live. Consequently, whether we are happy or sad, whether we are afflicted or consoled, whether everything is easy for us or whether we perceive ourselves to be utterly helpless, we must nourish our soul, we must live the interior life, we must unite ourselves to God.

There are times of famine when the poor, not finding food at home, go into the field and feed on herbs, roots, or any edible thing; they do all they can not to die of hunger. Likewise let us in times of desolation and helplessness, which are the famine periods, seek the way of uniting ourselves with God in spite of everything, in order that our interior life may not become extinguished or even lessened. Hence let us not anxiously inquire whether we are in a state of consolation or of desolation, whether God has already withdrawn Himself, whether He will return soon, and so on. Let us hold it as certain that our Lord gives us what we need moment by moment.

Do we lack knowledge of the state of our soul? Then of one thing we can be altogether sure: the present state of our soul is the most profitable for it at this very moment. God bestows on it whatever it needs at this moment. We should not eagerly seek after consolation or desolation, but only after the will of God, with the full assurance that at each moment His paternal providence sends us whatever we stand in need of, and that the best thing for us is to live the interior life continually, no matter what may be the circumstances in which we find ourselves.

9

In addition to knowing desolation, we ought to love it. Is not one of our duties to the cross, no matter what it may be, to love it and to embrace it? The attitude of St. Andrew toward the cross ought to be the attitude of every Christian soul, and like him, we ought to say to it: "Hail, precious cross, which has been so long a time desired and so intensely loved; receive in your arms the disciple of Him who effected His redemption on thee." To find our cross ought to be an occasion of joy for us, as it was for St. Andrew. If we knew the value of the cross, we would receive it with open arms, since it is Jesus Christ whom we receive on it.

Consequently we ought to accept afflictions with love and gratitude to the degree that we are capable, since they are a gift from God, a great grace. Ordinarily speaking, we receive consolations, sensible graces, and all pleasing things with thankfulness, and we believe that God sends them to us. Why, then, should we not receive these other and perhaps greater graces with the same gratitude, even though they are severe and pain-

ful? "If we have received good things at the hand
of God, why should we not receive evil?" [13] And
with greater reason, since they are evil only for
our bodies; for the soul they are favors, most precious favors.

As a general rule we ought to receive from
God's hand all that He sends us, without reflect-
ing on it and without regarding what He gives
us; and we ought to receive it with gratitude, for
the sole reason that He gives it to us. Let us suppose that our Lord should appear in our midst and
give to each one of us a wrapped package. I do
not know what is in my package. But is it not
true that even before knowing its contents I should
receive it with great gratitude for the simple
reason that He gives it to me and that it comes
impregnated with His love? This is the way we
should always comport ourselves with respect to
whatever Jesus ordains for us, and this is the way
we would conduct ourselves if we had faith. We
ought to accept each day as He sends it to us. It
is a sealed package that He gives us, and it comes
charged with His love. Why do we disquiet ourselves by asking whether today will be good or
bad, whether it will be joyful or sorrowful? One
thing ought to suffice us: the knowledge that Jesus
sends it to us, and that it is a testimony of His
love. Will today come with temptations, with
illnesses, with humiliations, with aridities? This

[13] Job 2:10.

matters little since it comes from God; that is enough. If we had faith!

Somewhere, either in history or in legend, I read that God once said to that doctor of the Middle Ages, Tauler, that He was going to give him a master of the spiritual life. Tauler was to go to a certain church, and there at the door he would find this master. Tauler went and encountered a miserable beggar covered with rags. He greeted him and bade him good day. The beggar answered him, assuring him that all his days were good, since God sent all of them to him. Tauler understood the deep spiritual doctrine which those words contained. Truly, all days are good; but we judge them with a human measuring-rod. One day pleases: what a precious day! Another disgusts us: what a miserable day! We err. All days are good since in each one of them God proffers the gift of His love, giving to us what is most apt for our sanctification.

If it were given to us to shape the day according to our caprice, what follies we would commit! For we would certainly arrange the day to our liking, and this would be the worst thing we could do. Which will be my best day? It will be precisely the one that our Lord sends me, since it will be neither defective nor excessive in anything. God has shaped it for me according to my precise needs. This is the way we ought to conform ourselves to the day that God sends us, and thus we shall live our spiritual life in the best possible manner.

If we ought to receive all crosses with love and gratitude, we ought to receive the more precious crosses with greater gratitude and greater love. If, in those packages which we spoke of, our Lord were to give us little crosses of ordinary wood, we should be grateful; but if the cross is not of common wood, but of the olive trees of Gethsemane, our gratitude ought to be greater; and if it should be made with particles of the true cross, then our gratitude should have no bounds.

Similarly, although all crosses are crosses, still some can be more precious than others. Although we ought to receive all as from the hand of God, yet we ought to receive the more precious ones with greater love and gratitude. Now, the most precious of these crosses are desolations. Hence we ought to receive them with the greatest love and gratitude.

There is a verse in the Psalms which seems strange upon first sight: "We have rejoiced for the days in which Thou hast humbled us: for the years in which we have seen evils." [14] No matter how strange this may seem, it is wholly true that in heaven above we shall rejoice exceedingly for all the days of our life. But the days that we shall recall with greatest love and gratitude will be the days on which our Lord humbled us and sent us

[14] Ps. 89:15.

desolation. Blessed desolation that came to purify and sanctify us! Precious are those days on which we suffered deeply, but on which our heart was transformed.

Such is the second thing that we ought to do in order to profit from desolations: we ought to receive them with love and gratitude, as every other thing that comes from the hands of God.

The third thing that we ought to do is to bear up under desolations. A cross is not given simply to be looked upon, but to be carried on one's shoulders. Hence when desolation comes, it is to be borne, not evaded. We must be determined to bear up under affliction. It is useless, as our Lord said to St. Paul, to kick against the goad; that is, it is useless and harmful to try to reject a cross that our Lord sends us. At least we ought to accept it with resignation. Our Lord is most considerate. He never sends us an affliction without our consent, and He asks it of us in one form or other. Have we not observed that at times, on a day of fervor, for example, our Lord knocks at our heart and then immediately we feel the need to commit ourselves to His will and to say: "Lord, I am disposed that You do whatever You will with me"? And then instantly comes some cross. Ordinarily speaking, we do not note the connection between the two; but in reality it is nothing else but the consent that God sought of us, and that He availed

Himself of instantly in order to send us the cross that was needful to sanctify us.

I would be sure of the result, should this be said to any soul suffering from desolation: "God has sent you this trial, and He wishes you to bear it; but if you do not wish to do so, there is a way of being relieved of it." I repeat that I am sure of the result, namely, that no soul would dare to say, "Yes, deliver me from it." We are not able to reject crosses without opposing the will of God. The least to do is to resolve to suffer, making a virtue of necessity. If we accept the trial willingly, so much the better. And if our acceptance is loving, wholehearted, and ardent, then it is best of all. To the degree that we accept desolations willingly, to that degree will they be profitable to us.

Even in human things it is better to suffer willingly than unwillingly. For example: when a person has a painful toothache, if instead of remaining quiet and patient under his pain, he moves about, becomes agitated, complains, loses heart, wanders to and fro, lies down, gets up, what is the result of all this? His nerves become more jumpy, and his pain becomes more intense. The reasonable thing is to remain quiet and to endure the pain until the time comes to see the dentist.

The same thing should be done in the spiritual order. Do we have a cross? Are we suffering from desolation? Let us endure it. "But I have no strength." That is not true; for our Lord has assured us that we shall never be tried beyond our strength. When He gives us a cross, He measures it out exactly. When we impose crosses on others, then, to be sure, strength may be lacking to support them. Sometimes superiors do not have the needed discretion, and they impose on the soul a cross that it cannot bear. But not so with our Lord. He computes our strength, or, better still, He bestows His graces in proportion to the crosses that He sends.

It is necessary, then, that when the soul is undergoing desolation it fail not in the fulfillment of its duties and in the living of its interior life. Let us recall this advice of St. Ignatius: "In time of desolation there must be no changing." This is a very practical counsel, since in time of desolation we desire to do everything exactly the opposite of how we do it in time of consolation. When a soul is enjoying consolation, the first thing it does is to prolong its prayer hour after hour; but when desolations come, then at once it wishes to shorten or to omit its prayer. No. In time of desolation there must be no change.

In the midst of desolation and despite it, we must live the interior life, perform our duties, adhere to our rules, carry out our exercises of piety: mortification, apostolic efforts, and so on, and be faithful to our Lord in our purposes and promises. Unquestionably all this will cost much at this time; but we must be generous. How much our Lord will be pleased if we comport ourselves thus in the midst of desolation!

Finally, what helps us most to profit from desolations is to cooperate with the action of God in whatever He proposes to achieve in us by them. In the event that God proposes to make us feel our misery through the force of desolation, let us unite ourselves to Him and open our eyes to see our nothingness and to take notice of our helplessness and weakness. He proposes also to exercise us in patience. Let us be generous in accepting the trial. He wishes a heart that is empty and free from created things, and a love that is most pure. Hence to the little extent that we can, let us enter into the purposes of God and second His designs.

How pleasing it will be to our Lord for us to enter into His very purposes, to second His divine action in our souls, even though what we can do may be very little!

10

Up to the present I have been considering desolation in its very essence, in its relation to our interior life; but I have not considered its circumstances and everything that goes with it. Let us not think that desolation resides only in the intimate part of our soul and that it affects only our interior life. As a rule desolation is attended with manifestations in all phases of our life, interior and exterior. Thus desolations do not always affect only the superior part of our soul with regard to our relations with God; ordinarily speaking, they are attended with other trials in the various faculties of our soul, and they have a connection even with external matters.

Some of these elements that accompany desolation are the natural consequence of it; others are added by our Lord that He may fully achieve in us His work of purification. Hence it is most profitable in times of desolation to have temptations and struggles and other difficulties that come from creatures. And certainly these states of the soul are the work of God; however, He not only works in the soul in a direct manner, but He also calls upon created things and uses them as His instruments.

The gifts of the Holy Ghost also intervene in a direct manner. It seems strange that these gifts which flood our soul with light, sweetness, and strength should serve at the same time as an instrument of immolation; but so it is. By means of His gifts the Holy Ghost accomplishes His work in souls.

To me it seems a certain delicacy on the part of our Lord to accord to creatures a partial role in the trials of desolation. He does not wish to assume the complete role in our immolation. Hence He does only what is indispensable; the rest He allows to creatures. And, marvelous to relate, He even uses the evil spirit in the purification of souls. This is not a frequent occurrence; but it does happen. When our Lord places a soul in the hands of the demon that he may try to torment it, naturally this is painful; it has a repugnant aspect, as do all things that come from the evil spirit. But to the demon's pride, how terrible it must be to see himself forced to serve his enemy, and to serve Him for his own defeat! It is as though in a war one of the combatants took a prisoner and forced him to build a military enclosure in which to kill his companions. I have spoken thus to make clear that all these things, which are apparently strange and foreign to desolation, are closely connected with it and serve to effect the purification that God desires in the soul.

I must make another observation. Even when the principal instruments that God uses to purify our souls in desolation are the intellectual gifts of knowledge and understanding, still the gift of fortitude also operates powerfully and exerts its influence that we may support all these trials and emerge victorious in all these struggles. At times our strength to resist astonishes us, and we ask ourselves: "How is it possible that I was able to bear up under all these things?" But the fact is that it is not I, but Jesus within me. He gives me the gift of fortitude, and with it I am capable of all things.

This truth should fill us with hope since, even though it is certain that we shall be obliged to suffer much, we can count on special helps and on the aid of our Lord, and with this aid we shall be able to triumph.

Let me summarize. What we must do in time of desolation is this: live in the obscurity of faith. In all the stages of the spiritual life we must live by faith; but in periods of desolation the specific remedy is the obscurity of faith. What does this mean? I shall explain myself. In times of desolation the soul is overwhelmed by darkness, seeing nothing. It sees neither God nor the road that leads to Him; and in a certain manner the soul does not even see itself, in the sense that it knows it is nothing. But in the midst of that complete darkness in which the soul lives, it is necessary that it go to God and that it travel the paths of the spiritual life, enlightened solely by faith, by a faith that is solitary, desolate, dark, black as night.

Let us open the works of St. John of the Cross and we shall meet with the same theme, the obscurity of faith. And, in truth, the great secret of the illuminative way consists in living in that obscurity of faith. But what is meant by living in the obscurity of faith? It means that we cling to what faith teaches us, although we neither perceive any joy or attraction in it, nor see its truth with clarity. At times we shall perceive a truth of faith with great clearness. How often it happens that of a sudden, we know neither how nor why, we understand most clearly a truth that we have heard many times before and understood only superficially. It appears as though we have had a revelation.

I remember a holy superior of a religious house who made a retreat by herself. When she finished it, she spoke to the community and said, "In this retreat I had a most clear light, as it were, a revelation." All the religious were eager to know what it was. "What was it that you saw, Mother?" they asked her. "Thou shalt love the Lord thy God with all thy heart, and thy neighbor as thyself." Is this a new thing, seeing that it is most ancient? Nevertheless at times we see with a new light those truths that are already well known. But we are unable to express what we feel and we see ourselves constrained to repeat the formula that is already twenty centuries old. Quite rightly can one exclaim: "What a great revelation!" "Thou shalt love the Lord thy God with thy whole heart, and thy neighbor as thyself." Assuredly, that is no new truth; but what is new is the depth with which we have seen it.

There are, then, times in which we see the most patent truths with the utmost clearness. At such moments faith is not an obscure faith; it is a faith that has about it a certain clarity. At other times we do not have clarity with which to penetrate divine truths, but an attraction toward them. On occasions we feel drawn toward a mystery of our Lord, to a text of Scripture, to some special virtue. If we ask ourselves how that is, we do not know the answer, yet we feel an attraction. We delight, for instance, in repeating and in savoring that text. This is faith. But it is not obscure; it is sweet since we feel that intimate attraction; we discover I know not what secrets that lie concealed in that text.

But when there is neither light nor attraction nor anything, when we utter an article of faith without understanding what faith teaches us, as when someone speaks a word in Russian or in Chinese, that is to live in the obscurity of faith.

I come to the foot of the tabernacle. I feel nothing. I have no enlightenment. It is as though I were in the public square. Absolutely nothing impresses me that Jesus is present; neither my heart nor my soul feels anything near the tabernacle. Nevertheless I say: "Here You are, Jesus. I adore You." And these words seem empty to me, and I feel nothing; but in the depth of my heart I believe, I love, I adore. That is to live in the obscurity of faith.

At other times Jesus manifests Himself in our daily life, and then we see Him in all things: in our neighbor, in the heavens, in events; our heart even trembles at the closeness of His presence.

This is faith, but it is not an obscure faith; it is a luminous faith, full of sweetness and delight.

Then there are other times when the veils that hide Jesus become more dense. We see nothing but defects in our neighbor; everything about him, from head to foot, grates on us. Events produce no other impression but that of despair, since everything turns out badly, as though our Lord were not at hand and as though He were allowing everything in this world to run wild. Everything is viewed with a desolating pessimism.

If at these times, despite everything, we see only God in the neighbor for the sole reason that faith teaches us God is there; if whatever we do is solely for Him; if in events, in spite of not seeing God, we have confidence in these words of His, "Not a single hair of your head will fall without the will of your Father who is in heaven," and if we persevere believing and believing, without seeing anything and without feeling anything, this is to live in the obscurity of faith. It is neither more nor less than if we were guided through a very obscure region by some person, and we followed his directions. "Now to the right," and we turn to the right. "Now straight ahead; now veer a little." And we keep doing whatever we are told solely because we are told; but as far as we are concerned there is nothing but darkness, and in the midst of it we travel with great misgiving, for it seems to us that at each step there is a precipice. That is to live in the obscurity of faith.

In time of consolation we walk, as it were, in a starlit night. There is not full darkness, simply a semi-obscurity. Hence when we see things, we do not see them very clearly. We see only well enough to get our bearings; and even then we make mistakes as we go along, and thus we step into water in the belief that we are placing our foot on a stone. But the time of desolation is like a black night, as when we walk in a cavern entirely shrouded in darkness, for then there is no recourse but to believe in him who guides us. We find this painful; for, although we are willing to suffer at the proper time, yet we wish to suffer with full knowledge of what we are undergoing; we wish to walk, but we should like to see our way. We are like those high ranking officers who upon their condemnation to death ask that as a special favor they may be allowed to direct their own execution, even to the point of saying, "Fire." They are killed, but beforehand they had the satisfaction of being the ones who arranged their own death.

We wish to know that we are suffering and that we are going to be immolated, but we ourselves also wish to be the ones to direct our immolation. Not to know where we are going is painful; but that is precisely the effect of leaving our own paths and entering into the ways of God. To arrive at transformation we must see with other eyes and love with another heart; and to see with other eyes we must pass through that darkness. After passing through that most dark passageway, we open our eyes, and now we no longer see as we saw before. We have a new way of seeing, of loving, and of understanding. In order to attain that, it was necessary for us to pass through such a dark passageway. In time of desolation and in time of consolation we must live by faith, but the obscurity of faith is more especially operative in periods of desolation.

Finally, when we are considering desolations that come from God, the most important thing to know is how the soul that finds itself in a state of desolation should act in order to make its prayer. Doctors sometimes use many medicines in treating the sick, but if there is a specific remedy, they give it the preference. For example, for swamp fever they can use arsenic; but quinine is the specific remedy. Similarly, there are many rules whereby we can put our spiritual organism in good condition and whereby we can dispose ourselves so that God may effect His work in us. But the specific is the prayer of desolation, that is, the prayer of the soul that suffers divine desolations.

How ought we to pray in time of desolation? In this time one of the most painful of things is prayer, and then all those moments in which we should place ourselves in immediate contact with our Lord are a torment. In the midst of work and of occupations, desolation is somewhat bearable; but upon placing ourselves in contact with God the torture grows. Tedium and sadness become most unbearable. And it is precisely at prayer that we perceive this in a special manner. We cannot keep up the continuity of it. Then what to do? Meditate? Impossible. The heart is like a stone from which not even the rod of Moses can draw forth the water of affections. Speak with our Lord? Nothing occurs to our mind to say to Him. Often sleep comes to solve the difficulty; but this is not the desirable solution.

St. John of the Cross teaches us what we are to do: simply look upon our Lord. It is very easy to prescribe this remedy; but how difficult it is to use it! I am going to explain it. This recipe means that we are not to seek this or that method to pray, since our tendency is to search out new means and new ways, and in the present state of the soul all that is useless. St. John of the Cross tells us this: "Do not busy yourself; let books and discourses alone, and everything else. The only thing that you are capable of is this: a looking upon God." But, holy Doctor! to look upon God? If we knew where He is! Is not that our desire and at the same time our torture and our pain?

But it is not absolutely certain that we do not know where God is. We know because we have faith: we know where He is, and we know the road to Him. Faith tells us that He is in the tabernacle, that He is in our heart. Then let us look upon the road that faith points out to us. That is the only thing we can do; that is what God wishes us to do, to look upon the road.

When the apostles saw our Lord ascend into heaven from the summit of Mount Olivet until a cloud hid Him from their sight, the Gospel tells us that they remained looking in the direction in which Jesus disappeared from view. And that was a natural thing to do. We must do the same: keep our eyes on the path. Where do we encounter Jesus on days of consolation except in the tabernacle and in our heart? Then let the gaze of our spirit penetrate to our heart; then let it turn to the tabernacle.

But this objection will be made to me. "Fine, but what do we gain by fixing our attention on the road? Is it something profitable?" Certainly it is. It is thought in time of desolation that prayer cannot be made; but such a view is false. Certainly it is made. What occurs is this: we do not realize it. How often a person who has spent time in prayer has experienced this truth: seeming to do nothing at prayer, nevertheless he emerges from it comforted and encouraged. And this seems extraordinary to him; he has done nothing, and yet he emerges a new being. Prayer that is made in time of desolation which comes from God is exactly the same as that made in time of consolation, which is so intimate and sweet. Have we not experienced at least occasionally how our soul fixes itself on God; how we need neither discourses, nor affections, nor anything; how we gaze on God and how He gazes upon us; how our soul becomes quieted, and how a sweet peace floods our heart?

Well then, that prayer is exactly the same as the prayer we make in time of desolation, with this sole difference: in the first case it is pleasant, and in the second case it is without feeling. It is so devoid of feeling that we do not know what we are accomplishing; yet we are praying. The important thing is, not to allow our spirit to wander to and fro. Quiet! Watch the road! If we fix our gaze on the road, we shall see more intensely what we wish to see. There will be a gazing in our heart that will escape our conscious knowledge, one that we cannot analyze, but that nevertheless encounters our Lord. It is the gaze of faith which finds out God even in the midst of shadows.

This is what we must do during prayer when we are suffering desolation: keep our eyes fixed on the road. If at some time we have enjoyed sweet tranquil prayer, let us strive to recapture it; let us do without joy and pleasure what we do with joy and pleasure on days of consolation. Whoever has experienced such prayer will know how to make his prayer when he is desolate: not, of course with sweetness, but with the same care and ingenuousness. If any feeling enters in that simple gaze upon God, it seems to me that it should be an utter self-abnegation in the presence of God and an abandonment to Him: "I am nothing, but I place myself at Your disposition. Here I am."

I am going to make a comparison that is a bit prosaic, but I do not resist the inclination to make it since it appears to me to be apposite. When we were children we were told this story. A person entered into heaven, escaping the vigilance of the Apostle St. Peter. When the saint noticed the person, he said to him. "Be thou turned into stone." "Yes, St. Peter," said the intruder, "but with eyes." He was turned into a stone, but with eyes in order that he might see everything that was taking place in heaven. It seems to me that something similar takes place in a soul that suffers desolation. Such a soul is like a hard, cold stone, but with eyes. How often have we described our state by saying, "I am like a stone"! In this state we can at least see; the eyes of our desolated soul are the eyes of faith, and with these eyes we can fix our gaze on the road. In the final analysis, the secret, the specific remedy, for passing through periods of desolation is the same as the one I gave for living the spiritual life: live by faith.

I have explained the two secrets that are, as it were, the key of the spiritual life: to live in the obscurity of faith, and to understand that the ways of God are different from our ways. Consequently we ought not to wish to travel by our ways, but to accustom ourselves to travel by the paths of God. At the moment of pain and tribulation rules of spirituality will not occur to the mind, or they will seem to have no efficacy in the soul. There is, however, another teaching, the teaching of God, which always sinks into our souls and enlightens us in the midst of darkness and strengthens us in the midst of tribulations. May this teaching resound in our hearts, and may the hidden, mysterious, but always efficacious light of God, lighten our way in times of affliction, that we may be faithful to God and thus bring to perfection His divine designs on our souls.

X

The Role of Contemplatives

▲▲

The world does not understand saints; much
less does it understand contemplatives. "What
purpose do they serve?" it says with disdain. If
it were for nothing more than aesthetic reasons,
there ought to be contemplatives in the world.
What purpose do they serve? They serve the same
purpose as flowers: to perfume the air with their
fragrance and to gladden the sight with their
lovely colors. They serve the same purpose as the
stars: to fill our nights with enchantment. They
serve the purpose that everything beautiful serves,
that everything noble serves, and that everything
holy serves: namely, to remind us that we are not
born for this world; to tell us, in the midst of the
tribulations, sorrows, and annoyances of this life,
that we are above them and that we have been
born for higher things; to keep us mindful of the
truth that there is an everlasting home in which
a Father awaits us with outstretched arms of love,
and in which a Mother offers us rest and peace

with her fond and endearing reception. Contemplatives are the heralds of the eternal fatherland,
the messengers of divine love. When they draw
near to us, we feel that the scented zephyrs of
the promised land are approaching to refresh our
brows in the barren wastes of this world. When
they speak, we might say that we hear a prelude
of the heavenly canticles. To look upon them is to
enjoy a radiant vision from heaven; they have
about them something that is angelic, heavenly,
divine.

Only a few contemplatives would suffice to
make us forget all the crimes and all the misfor-
tunes of humanity; to make us proud of our line-
age; to convince us that God exists, and that God
is love. If for no other than for aesthetic reasons,
contemplatives should be; and the aesthetic order
is the order of divinity.

Contemplatives also exercise a stabilizing role
in the world. On the day when the equilibrium of
the heavenly bodies would be broken, the world
would perish in a terrible catastrophe. On the day
when the mysterious balance between good and
evil would exist no longer, when evil would really
and definitively overcome good, then an even
more terrible catastrophe would come to pass.

But the hand of God preserves the balance in
both worlds. When the equilibrium threatens to
be upset in any part of the firmament, God sends
those wandering and mysterious stars that visit

our heavens from time to time, in order to re-establish it. When evil extends itself over the earth and seems to subjugate souls, when the seeds of error and iniquity appear on the point of producing an explosion and of hurling the human race into the abyss, then God draws out from the treasures of His mercy and of His love His saints, especially His contemplatives, and sends them upon the earth as a pledge of peace, as a smile of mercy. Then the contemplatives flash across the heaven of the Church, wandering and mysterious like comets, radiating like them both beauty and light. They come to re-establish the balance; they come to announce peace.

The epochs of catastrophes are the epochs of contemplatives. When the Western Schism was splitting the Church, St. Vincent Ferrer and St. Catherine of Siena shone in the world. The age of Protestantism is the age of St. John of the Cross and of St. Theresa of Avila, the age of saints. And when the bloody beginnings of the French Revolution appeared in history, Jesus revealed the treasures of His heart by means of the sweet Visitation Sister of Paray-le-Monial.

The saints ever save the world. The great law of the vicariousness of merits, proclaimed in the Book of Genesis, is of perpetual application: "I will not destroy it [Sodom] for the sake of ten." [1]

[1] Gen. 18:32.

Woe to the world on the day on which it will not have in its midst the number of just demanded by mercy! On that day it will be consumed without fail by the fire of justice.

Without doubt all the saints have this mission of cooperating in the work of Jesus, the Lamb of God who takes away the sins of the world. But I maintain that this role is the more fitting and, after a manner of speaking, the specific role of the contemplatives. Action and contemplation save the world, but in different ways. Action goes to God through the medium of men; contemplation comes to men from God.

Contemplation is the glory of God in the souls of the saints; action is the radiations of that glory which are cast abroad in the world. Contemplation is the fragrance of the holocaust that ascends to the heavens, swift and triumphant; action is the sweetness of that fragrance which is spread abroad over the earth. Contemplation is the portion of God, His first fruits, as it were, the marrow of the amount that He reserves for Himself; action is the portion of men, the crumbs that God allows to fall from His magnificent banquet. Action is of the earth; contemplation is of heaven.

"The contemplative life," says St. Thomas, "is according to divine things, whereas active life is according to human things; wherefore Augustine says: 'In the beginning was the Word; to Him was Mary hearkening: The Word was made flesh: Him was Martha serving.' " [2]

God makes use of action to effect His work upon earth: by means of action He enlightens, warms, cures, strengthens, and consoles men. Contemplation He reserves for Himself, for His repose, and for His delight. It is the garden in which He takes His pleasure, the Bethany where He rests, the sanctuary of His peace, the cradle of His loves, the throne of His glory, His heaven on earth.

The gaze of God, rather of His love than of His power, sustains the world. The day on which He shall avert His eyes, the world will sink. But this gaze needs a place whereon to rest; it needs an oasis in the desert of this world, which is dry, burning, shaken by the devastating hot dust storm of evil. This oasis is contemplation; on it the gaze of love finds its rest, and the waters that spring up there are capable of changing the desert into paradise.

Contemplatives are God's resounding trumpets. God has two methods of teaching. One is solemn and official, of which the teaching Church is the organ; the other is intimate and loving, which, as a rule, God conveys to the contemplatives. The time of public revelations closed with the Apocalypse; but private revelations will continue till the end of the world. There is no question

[2] *Summa theol.*, IIa IIae, q. 182, a. 1.

that these latter do not have the force of the former; nor do they have any worth without the approbation of the Church. But when they obtain it, how much light and love are diffused over the earth! What prodigious richness they possess! How potent they are to renew the world! To understand this, we need only consider the marvels effected by the secret words which were placed by Jesus in the heart of Margaret Mary and the firm hope which they engender.

These revelations are a most loving and devotional commentary on the teaching of the Church. They are the finger of God which points out to dull and forgetful men the treasure they possess without appreciating it, and the truths they know without understanding them. They come to emphasize certain divine teachings and certain divine gifts which can save the world, but which the world does not understand or has forgotten. They come to cast abroad on the earth the spark of love that consumes hearts and reanimates souls.

Here is a notable thing worthy to be studied by those who have the ability to explain it. The great devotions of the Church, those that make history, those that descend upon the earth like a smile from heaven, announcing peace in the hour of catastrophe (such as the devotion to the Eucharist in the Middle Ages, and the devotion to the Cross in ages even more remote) have not sprung up in the Church through the direct initiative of the official hierarchy; they germinated in the hearts of the faithful. God placed the seed in the soul of His saints, as a rule in the soul of His contemplatives, and nearly always in the heart of a woman.

The gifts of God, the marvels of His love that come down from heaven, descend upon the members of the Church, first by diffusing themselves on the head, then by flowing downward from there to the faithful, as an unction of mercy passing over the beard of Aaron and impregnating with its sweetness even the fringe of his mantle. Devotion is the simple offering of human love that corresponds in its way to the divine gifts; it is the echo of love that the ineffable word of the Bridegroom awakens in the heart of the beloved; it is the living flame of love that rises from earth to heaven. Perhaps for this reason it takes an opposite course on the pathway through which the gifts of God descend to us. It arises in the members, free and spontaneous as love; and flaming like it, it mounts to the heights. But first it must pass through the head of the Church, who alone can accept and bless human gifts in the name of God and offer them to the Lord in the name of His children.

Be this as it may, let it suffice for me to call attention to the fact, which is indisputable and of consuming interest. Contemplatives are the repositories of the secrets of God, the heralds of His intimate and loving teaching.

Let us leave the world that smiles at the saints and asks with disdain: "To what purpose are contemplatives?" Its eyes are obscured by shadows, its heart is cold, its spirit is the spirit of falseness. Let us who have received the Spirit of God say, filled with wonder and with love, along with the Psalmist, "God is wonderful in his saints." [8]

[8] Ps. 67:36.

XI

Spiritual Marriage

Nothing so enkindles the love of God as the
realization of His particular benefits, as St.
Thomas and St. Francis of Sales teach. Indeed,
what else is more apt to produce love than love
itself? The divine chains with which God attracts
and binds souls are the chains of love, according
to the words of Osee: "I will draw them with the
cords of Adam, with the bands of love."[1] And
what are the benefits that we have received from
God but the gifts of the Holy Ghost, and trials,
which are the effects of His love?

Let not souls that have been raised to the
heights of the mystic life be fearful; let them
reflect without trepidation, and examine with love
the graces the Lord has bestowed on them. Humility is not endangered by this; rather the opposite is true, since a recognition of the divine
beneficences increases and intensifies it. Humility
is light, and it is nourished by light; since every
grace of God is luminous, every grace from God

[1] Osee 11:4.

181

increases humility. This virtue is also intimately bound up with love. Indeed, one might say that to a certain degree it is love itself. How, then, can humility encounter danger with that which serves as an incentive to love?

God's most humble creature, after the holy humanity of Christ, is the Blessed Virgin, the one who has understood better than anyone else the immensity of the blessings she received from God. Her Magnificat is a canticle of humility as well as of gratitude and love. The Virgin herself is the author of her own panegyric, one that has never been surpassed by creatures, glorifying God and rejoicing in her Savior, because He has done great things in her, He who is mighty and whose name is holy. Furthermore, does not experience teach that all God's favors humble, confound, and abase? This self-abasement is the very essence of humility, love, and adoration.

Nor need privileged souls be too greatly concerned about not corresponding to grace. To be sure, if anyone looks upon his own nothingness, there is great reason to fear; but if he fixes his gaze on the goodness and the love of God, what is there to fear? God gives "both to will and to accomplish"; yes, even the correspondence with grace is a gift of God. The soul that confides in Him will never be confounded, and He who enriches the soul with the treasures of His love will cause the soul to know how to profit from them.

Let not the espoused soul be fearful; her exaggerated fear will be displeasing to the divine Spouse. Let her place in Him an absolute confidence, unlimited and unwavering. Is He not able to protect her, even against her own baseness? He is sufficiently powerful, and He loves her too much to allow her to be unfaithful. Let her abandon herself completely to Him: to His will, to His graces, to His love. Let her engrave deeply in her soul that golden motto from the Psalms: "Cast thy care upon the Lord, and He shall sustain thee." [2] Cast upon Him even that care which seems so proper, that of being faithful to Him; and God will take care of everything. Let her place in God's hands even her own correspondence with grace; let her make Him accountable; let her make Him responsible for the use she ought to make of divine favors. Then He will take care of everything, since her confidence impels Him.

In speaking of marriage, St. Paul says that it is a great sacrament, since it represents the indissoluble union between Christ and the Church. "This is a great sacrament; but I speak in Christ and in the Church." [3] And St. Thomas adds: "in God and the soul."

Among men, marriage is the symbol of that divine union which God condescends to effect with souls. Every soul was created to be the spouse

[2] Ps. 54:23.
[3] Ephes. 5:32.

of the divine Word, and that ineffable union in heaven, which is the basis of our hope, is nothing else but the mystery of our eternal espousals with the Word.

God, in the holy impatience of His love, does not wait for death in order to unite Himself with certain privileged souls whom He loves with a special love. He begins on earth the heavenly espousals, and He unites Himself with those chosen souls, not in the complete and perfect way of heaven, yet in so intimate, so sweet, and so permanent a manner that this union is the beginning and the prelude to the consummate union of heaven.

No union on earth is more intimate than the union of the spiritual marriage. Earthly comparisons that are used to explain it are wholly inadequate. Neither the drop of water that is lost in the ocean, nor the pieces of wax that have been fused together, nor anything else, can give an idea of this union that makes the eternal Word and the soul one. The only exact, though ineffable, comparisons are: the union of human nature with the divine in the person of the Word, and the union of the Father and the Son and the Holy Ghost in the supreme oneness of the divine substance.

Spiritual marriage is, as it were, the extension of the mystery of the Incarnation to souls, and it is also a participation in the august mystery of the

Trinity. God celebrated the eternal espousals with human nature by uniting Himself hypostatically with the human nature of Christ in the womb of Mary; by reason of that admirable union Christ is truly the Son of God.

The Word does not unite Himself with other souls hypostatically; nevertheless He does unite Himself to them in a very close and very exalted union which is similar to the hypostatic union, and which flows from it inasmuch as it is through Christ that souls are united to the Word. From that union there results, not a begotten son, but sons according to adoption. Adoptive sonship begins on earth and is consummated in heaven. Through spiritual marriage souls have on earth a foretaste of the perfect adoption of heaven.

This marriage is also a participation in the mystery of the Blessed Trinity. The soul is united with the Word. I shall say nothing of this union. May the soul perceive it and relish it in silence. Let her no longer seek her Beloved, nor ask of the heavens and of the earth, as did the spouse of the Canticle of Canticles, "Have you seen him, whom my soul loveth?" Or as St. John of the Cross beautifully paraphrases this verse:

> "O woods and thickets
> Planted by the hand of the Beloved!
> O meadow of verdure, enamelled with flowers,
> Say if he has passed by you." [4]

[4] Cant. 3:3. *Spiritual Canticle*, v. 3.

She has Him; she possesses Him in the innermost depth of her being. Let her say rather as
the spouse of the Canticles said: "I found him
whom my soul loveth: I held him: and I will not
let him go." [5] "I to my beloved, and my beloved
to me."

This union with the Word is lasting and not
transient as in other states. The Spouse is faithful,
and nothing, not even death, will be able to break
this most binding union. For those who are bound
to the Word in this way, these heavenly words
of St. Paul apply: "For I am sure that neither
death nor life . . . shall be able to separate us
from the love of God, which is in Christ Jesus
our Lord." [6]

Happy the soul that has already tasted the
sweetness, the ineffable sweetness, of this union
and that has been admitted into the dwelling place
of the Beloved and there has been enraptured
and overwhelmed with love! To the soul thus
united with the Word the secrets of God are revealed, and her prayers possess a most singular
power in the divine heart.

It is even granted to the body to feel the heavenly effect of that union. Ecstasies now become
rarer because the soul has become one in nature,
so to say, with divine things. Concupiscence is
overcome and stands completely subject to the

[5] Cant. 3:4.
[6] Rom. 8:38 f.

soul. And how many times even the flesh participates in the joy of the spirit, thus confirming that verse from the Psalms: "My heart and my flesh have rejoiced in the living God." [7]

United thus intimately, sweetly, and permanently with the Word, the soul participates in the very life of God and enters with the other Persons of the adorable Trinity into the same relations as they have with the Word.

The Father gazes at the soul with that unique, infinite, eternal, and most fruitful gaze with which He engendered the Word, "in the brightness of the saints . . . before the day star." [8] What a gaze of complacency, what a gaze of love, what a marvelous gaze that engenders new life!

The gaze of God peoples nothingness with beings; the gaze of God makes the earth tremble when it is fixed upon it. "He looketh upon the earth, and maketh it tremble." [9] The regard of God was sufficient to make Mary so joyful that all generations will call her blessed. "Because He hath regarded the humility of His handmaid . . . all generations shall call me blessed." [10] That regard of the Father upon the soul that is united with the Word is sufficient to melt the soul with tenderness and to cause it to foretaste in the wilderness the anticipated joy of heaven.

[7] Ps. 83:3.
[8] Ps. 109:3.
[9] Ps. 103:32.
[10] Luke 1:48.

And in this divine marriage, what is the dowry that the Spouse gives to His bride? It is the Holy Ghost, the eternal and consubstantial love of God. He is the Spirit of the Word connaturally, and He becomes the Spirit of the soul by participation, as the Scriptures say: "But he who is joined to the Lord, is one spirit." [11]

This Spirit strengthens the soul so that it may be able to bear the union with the Most High; He beautifies it so that it may be worthy of the divine Spouse; He overshadows it in a manner like that by which He overshadowed Mary in the solemn moment of the Incarnation. And this divine Spirit is also the bond, the most loving bond that unites the soul with the Word, consuming the soul with heavenly love.

The soul's master, its interior director, its most faithful guide is the Holy Ghost. To fulfill the designs of God, to unfold that very intense life which the soul already possesses, it need do nothing more than allow itself to be led by Him, follow His suggestions, and let itself be moved by His tender and powerful inspiration; and all this at one and the same time. What can the soul fear in His hands? It abandons itself, it gives way without resistance, without fear. It can do all things in Him that strengthens it. O happy and most perfect state! God communicates to the soul His torrents, His light. Now He reveals to it His secrets,

[11] I Cor. 6:17.

now He communicates to it His attributes; at another time He discloses to it a little of the mystery of life; then again He introduces it into that divine darkness where God dwells and in which it learns something of God through a sublime ignorance, knowing that God is incomprehensible and that He is infinitely above every created thing.

The intellect is enlightened and the will is most sweetly touched and caressed by Divinity. O most delightful union! O true embraces and kisses of the Spouse! O happy realization of that daring and supreme desire of the Bride of the Canticle of Canticles: "Let him kiss me with the kiss of his mouth." [12]

The fruit of that marriage is the formation of Christ in the soul, to make her a living image of Jesus. And once the soul is transformed into Christ, she will be like the divine Master: powerful in words and in works to accomplish on earth the task that God has destined her to.

Let not the soul be fearful at being called by the greatest titles and the sweetest names by the divine Spouse. Let her humble herself. Let her blush with the holy and most delicate blush of love; but let her not be fearful because she is nothing. It is precisely for that reason that God takes her as the instrument of His marvels. That is God's way. "The foolish things of the world hath God chosen, that He may confound the wise;

[12] Cant. 1:1.

and the weak things of the world hath God chosen, that He may confound the strong. And the base things of the world, and the things that are contemptible, hath God chosen, and things that are not, that He might bring to nought things that are; that no flesh should glory in His sight." [13]

Let her not be frightened at hearing herself being called Bride. She is truly that in view of the incomprehensible love of God. Let her rejoice and savor the sweetness of that name in humility and in love.

Let her not be frightened at hearing herself being called Delight and Rest and Sanctuary. She is a delight because she is a bride. Whose duty is it but the bride's to delight the Spouse with her tenderness? Where is the Spouse to seek for repose if not in the heart of the bride, who has been transformed by Him into an abode of love, into a garden enclosed where the most exquisite fruits are cultivated and where the richest flowers diffuse their fragrance? This garden is the Spouse's very own, because He planted it; it is His own because He waters it, cultivates it, and preserves it. It is His own because it is for Him alone. Let the soul invite Him as the bride of the Canticle of Canticles, saying to Him as she burns with love and desire: "Let my beloved come into his garden, and eat the fruit of his apple trees." [14]

[13] I Cor. 1:27–29.
[14] Cant. 5:1.

And because she is the sanctuary of the heart of Christ, she is also an asylum for sinners; for God has not enriched her soul with so many graces for her sake alone, but also for the good of her brethren. Let her use these graces in praying; let her use them in loving: loving for those who do not love; adoring for those who do not adore; placating the justice of God for those who arouse it.

At the present time when evil is extending itself without restraint throughout the world; now when even we, who should know better, increase the suffering of the heart of Christ with our faults; let the espoused soul love; let her love intensely that Christ may not leave, that He may remain with us; let her say to Him with the beatings of her heart those sweet words of the disciples at Emmaus: "Stay with us, because it is toward evening, and the day is now far spent." [15]

I know the heart of God. It cannot resist love. Even though He might wish to go, He would not do so if His spouses would detain Him, enchain Him, imprison Him with the irresistible bands of love. His justice impels Him to separate Himself from us. But since He loves us, He does not wish to go; and He Himself has enkindled His love in many souls in order that they might detain Him, that they might not let Him go. Oh, the tenderness of His love! Oh, the ingenious devices of His mercy! Away with fears! Let the espoused

[15] Luke 24:29.

soul come into the presence of God with the holy audacity of love. Let her hold fast to Him; let her do Him violence; let her struggle with Him, if it be necessary, like Jacob; and she will conquer, because love is as strong as death.

Here are two concluding remarks. In the first place, the soul merits with the acts of contemplation in all its forms. What happiness to merit one heaven with another! Let the soul give herself to love without reserve and without fear; for the more she gives herself and the more perfectly she loves, the more will she merit for herself and for others. Love merits most because charity is the queen of the virtues and the bond of perfection.

Secondly, let the soul in this state give herself without fear to the desire for blessedness, to the sweet martyrdom of love which the communications with God, and especially the divine unions, produce in the soul. They hurt her, wound her, and cause her to sigh and groan for the perfect possession of the Beloved. This disposition is very perfect, especially if she joins with this most ardent desire the heroic act of conforming herself to the will of God, and even of asking Him to prolong her exile, as long as He might will, for His glory and for the good of souls.

XII

Transformation into God

According to St. Bernard, St. Thomas, and St. John of the Cross, this transformation is the final stage of love; consequently it is the summit of holiness. This degree is so exalted that it is proper to heaven. However, God in His mercy and in His love concedes it to some privileged souls on earth. Love is union or a tendency to union. Infinite love is the most perfect union; created love tends to union on earth, and in heaven it will achieve the most perfect union which it is capable of, the perfect participation of the all-holy and the all-blessed oneness of God.

To be transformed into God, to be transformed into the Beloved, is to begin to enjoy in this life that union with God which constitutes the holiness, the glory, and the blessedness of the saints. This is the consummation of the union that Christ prayed for to His Father with most ardent desires and petitions on the night of the Last Supper: "I in them, and Thou in Me; that they may be made perfect in one." [1] This is also what the Holy Ghost asks for with unspeakable groanings in the souls of those He loves.[2]

What is it that the espoused soul seeks, what is it that she sighs for when she feels hunger and thirst, and when she suffers sharp pain in her excruciating martyrdom of love? What is it that she yearns for but the consummation of this union?

"If you are conformed to My will, if you are in this union, and if all that is Mine is yours, what more do you wish?" This is what our Lord can say to her.

"I wish for more," answers the soul: "more love, more suffering, more knowledge, more union. I wish for the consummation of unity."

Love is inexhaustible. In its vocabulary the word "enough" is not found. It has been replaced by this word, "more." "They that eat me, shall yet hunger; and they that drink me, shall yet thirst." [3] Love is like that: the greater the repletion, the greater the hunger; the greater the satiety, the greater the thirst.

How is this transformation to be accomplished? Everything in the soul must become divine; everything must be changed into the living image of Christ. The Word became hypostatically united

[1] John 17:23.
[2] Cf. Rom. 8:26.
[3] Ecclus. 24:29.

to the most sacred humanity of Christ; through the grace of the spiritual marriage the Word becomes united, in an ineffable manner, to the humanity of the espoused soul. What does that divine Word desire? He desires that His adopted humanity become more and more assimilated to His personal humanity; that is, that the humanity of His beloved become the image of the humanity of Christ: in her soul, in her heart, in her character, and even in her flesh.

"And when the similarity will be perfect, the union will be so also; and when the humanity which is I, shall appear in glory, then that which is you will also appear, together with all those who are your brethren. And then that which you call your ideal will be seen fully realized, and which could not have been your ideal except that it was My design, namely, "Christ is all, and in all," [4] and "all things united into one through Christ." [5]

The espoused must be similar to Christ in her soul through a most elevated and most intimate union with the Word of God; a union already exists, but the Word asks for a greater union.

The espoused must be similar to Christ in her heart. The heart of Christ is love and sorrow. His heart, like all that He is, is white and ruddy, according to the words of the bride in the Canticle

[4] Col. 3:11.
[5] Gay, *Elevations*, II, 394.

of Canticles; [6] white because it is the brightness of eternal light,[7] ruddy because it is crimsoned with His most precious blood. The heart of Christ is composed of love and of the sorrow which His two great and consuming passions have produced: namely, the glory of God and the salvation of souls. Thus ought to be the heart of the espoused soul.

She must also be like Christ in her character, which is meek and humble. "Learn of Me, because I am meek, and humble of heart." [8] Her words, her actions, her deportment, her exterior conduct ought to breathe that charming humility and that heavenly meekness of Christ. And this ought to be to such an extent that men would discern Christ whenever they would approach her, since she would be diffusing the good odor of Christ on all sides and attracting everyone with the fragrance of her perfumes.

Finally, the espoused soul must be similar to Christ in her flesh. "Always bearing about in our body the mortification of Jesus, that the life also of Jesus may be made manifest in our bodies. For we who live are always delivered unto death for Jesus' sake; that the life also of Jesus may be made manifest in our mortal flesh." [9] In this way she

[6] Cant. 5:10.
[7] Wisd. 7:26.
[8] Matt. 11:29.
[9] II Cor. 4:10 f.

is akin to the afflicted body of Christ on earth
until the day comes when she will be like His
glorious body in heaven, according to that text of
St. Paul: "We look for the Savior, our Lord Jesus
Christ, who will reform the body of our lowness,
made like to the body of His glory." [10]

Only one phase of this transformation will be
accomplished on earth: the transformation of sorrow, since earth is the place of sorrow. In heaven
the most intimate of all unions will be realized
in joy. On earth the most intimate union is that
of sorrow. This will be effected on earth; the other
will find its consummation only in heaven. For
this reason St. Theresa used to say: "Aut pati aut
mori"; either to suffer in order to be united with
Christ in the most intimate of unions on earth,
which is the union of sorrow, or to die in order
to be united with Christ in heaven in the most
perfect union of everlasting joy.

However, in a most exalted sense the union of
sorrow is, perhaps, to be met with in heaven, in
some mysterious consummation or other. When
His mortal life ended, did the heart of Christ lose
the abyss of its sorrows? Did its essence change?
Did it cease to be the white and ruddy fusion of
love and of sorrow? In heaven and in the Eucharist
the sorrow of Christ is incomprehensible, tran-
scendental, and mysterious in manner; and it is

[10] Phil. 3:20 f.

sorrow. In heaven the Lamb is as it were immolated. "And I saw . . . a Lamb standing as it were slain." [11]

The Eucharist is a sacrifice, a mysterious and ineffable immolation, but none the less an immolation. It is the multiplication in space and the perpetuation in time of the love and of the sorrow of Christ. This we can see, in the words of the Apocalypse quoted above, what might be called the Eucharist of heaven: the perpetuation in eternity of that same sorrow of Christ, a glorified sorrow, a triumphant sorrow, a jubilant sorrow, a sorrow purified of everything earthly, a sorrow that plunges into the ocean of love and merges with eternal joy. This transformation into God is, moreover, intimately bound up with the missions that God is accustomed to confide to the espoused soul.

Monsignor Gay has some admirable pages that throw much light on this point. The matter is in the form of a dialogue.

"Lord, what do You wish me to do?"

"Is it not first necessary to know what I wish you to be? Is it not necessary to be before one can act?"

"Well, then, Lord, that I may conform myself more closely to Your will and merit to be pleasing to You, what do You wish me to be?

"Simply be Jesus."

[11] Apoc. 5:6.

The soul is astonished, considers her lowliness, her sins, her imperfection; doubts and fears assail her. Jesus deigns to instruct the soul and to clear away all her difficulties.

"You do not understand love very well."

"Master, teach it to me. I am most desirous to learn this science and especially to learn it of You."

Christ enlightens the soul. She is filled with joy and with wonder, and in the midst of her felicity she exclaims:

"O love, thou art not known!"

"I am unknown," answers Jesus; "and I am despised."

"Beloved master! if You are unknown, manifest Yourself; if You are despised, take away the shame. O unknown love, send forth preachers; O despised love, raise up souls to make reparation! Since You are unknown, we need apostles; since You are despised, we need victims."

And then the soul understood that the holy humanity of Him whom she adores had been both of these things with respect to love: that He had manifested and preached Himself during life, and that He had made complete reparation through His death.

Now indeed this incomparable Master was showing and explaining to the soul that this same work is continued by Him, and that He even wishes to do it through His members. And only

He can accomplish it. This is so true that only by incorporating herself into Him through sanctifying grace, and by entering into Him through love in order to identify herself with Him in the unity of the Holy Ghost, can she hope to serve love usefully; that is, announce Him to the world, and at the same time make reparation to Him for the world. And this practically amounts to the first words that our Lord had deigned to say, namely: "Be Jesus by living the life of Jesus, in order to do the work of Jesus." [12]

O God, deign to transform more perfectly into Jesus the soul with whom the Word has united Himself, that she may do the work of Jesus, that she may be an apostle and a victim of love, and that she may obtain of God with her prayers and her sacrifices that the apostles and the victims of love may be increased.

"The secret of becoming Jesus is to allow Jesus a free hand. Jesus is the only one who can effect a continuation of His life upon earth; the members of Christ need do nothing more than "to cling to Him firmly, and to maintain themselves in Him, generous, humble, and free of self-love, acquiescing to all His designs, submitting themselves to all His influences, following all His movements, working under His direction." [13]

This is the work of God; this is chiefly the work

[12] Gay, *Elevations*, II, 437.
[13] *Ibid.*

of the Holy Ghost. Is not the formation of Christ in the womb of Mary attributed to this divine Spirit? He is also the one who forms Him in souls. There is unity in the works of God. The soul cannot but say with the Blessed Virgin Mary: "Behold the handmaid of the Lord; be it done to me according to thy word." [14] This ought to be the divine formula with which the soul responds to our Lord when He has any design upon her. No delays; no postponements. The only response that is proper for a soul with respect to God, the only reply that is worthy of a bride when her Spouse calls her, is this one: "Yes. So be it! Let it be done!"

The espoused soul no longer has a will of her own; she no longer has her own judgment; her will is the will of the Beloved, and her judgment is the judgment of the Spouse. What if she is imperfect, lowly, nothing? She should not fix her attention on that; her rule is the will of the Beloved, and nothing else. Does He call her? Let her open to Him. Does He wish to accomplish marvels in her? Let her say to him with love, and adoration, and abandonment: "Behold the handmaid of the Lord; be it done to me according to thy word."

And we must not forget that wherever Christ is, He is formed by the Holy Ghost; and that wherever Christ is, He is also, and for the same reason, conceived in a certain manner by the

14 Luke 1:38.

Blessed Virgin Mary. Let the soul call upon that most tender Mother; let the soul invoke her that with her powerful intercession she may obtain the soul's perfect transformation into Christ. The espoused soul ought to ask for this transformation. It is pleasing to God that we ask for and desire the very grace that He wishes to give us, especially when this grace is that of union, when the gift that we beseech is He Himself.

Wherefore let the soul that is united with the Word ask with insistence from the Holy Ghost for this supreme grace, which is the highest degree of perfection and of holiness, the ultimate degree of union and of love, the supreme degree of happiness.

Index